Racial Conflict and the American Mayor

Racial Conflict and the American Mayor

Power, Polarization, and Performance

Charles H. Levine
Syracuse University

Lexington Books
D.C. Heath and Company
Lexington, Massachusetts
Toronto   London

Library of Congress Cataloging in Publication Data

Levine, Charles H.
   Racial conflict and the American mayor.

   1. Mayors—United States. 2. Mayors—United States—Case
studies. 3. United States—Race question—Case studies. I. Title.
JS363.L47   352'.0083'0973   73-11646
ISBN 0-669-90233-0

Published simultaneously in Canada.

Printed in the United States of America.

International Standard Book Number: 0-669-90233-0

Library of Congress Catalog Card Number: 73-11646

To My Two Elaines

Contents

List of Tables and Figures   ix

Preface   xi

Part I   *Introduction*   1

Chapter 1   **Racial Conflict and the Paradox of Mayoral Leadership**   3

    Objectives   5
    Methodology   6

Part II   *Racial Conflict and Models of Mayoral Leadership*   9

Chapter 2   **The Pluralist Model of Mayoral Leadership: An Overgeneralized Strategy for Limited Contexts**   11

    Mayoral Leadership as a Problem of Methodology   12
    The Dominant Model of Mayoral Effectiveness   14
    The Limits of Mayoral Leadership   21

Chapter 3   **Racial Conflict as a Constraint and an Opportunity for Mayoral Leadership**   35

    Conflict Patterns in Pluralized and Polarized Systems   37
    Mayoral Leadership as Bystandership, Partisanship, and Hegemonyship   41
    The Special Case of Consociation   43

Part III   *Mayoral Leadership in Three Racially Polarized Contexts*   51

Chapter 4   **Cleveland: The Politics of Immobilism**   53

    Background and Structure   53
    Electoral Politics   55
    Policy Politics and Leadership Structure   60
    Achievements and Failures   64

Chapter 5	**Gary: The Politics of Racial Partisanship**	69
	Background and Structure	69
	Electoral Politics	70
	Policy Politics and Leadership Structure	73
	Achievements and Failures	77
Chapter 6	**Birmingham: The Politics of Hegemony**	85
	Background and Structure	85
	Electoral Politics	89
	Policy Politics and Leadership Structure	94
	Achievements and Failures	98
Part IV	*Conclusion*	107
Chapter 7	**Racial Conflict and the Future of the American Mayor: Lessons from Cleveland, Gary, and Birmingham**	109
	Contextual Characteristics	109
	Formal and Informal Power	113
	Effectiveness and Policy Impact	114
	Racial Conflict and the Future of the American Mayoralty	115
Chapter 8	**Toward a Contingency Theory of Mayoral Effectiveness**	127
	The Sociology of Political Knowledge and the Administrative Science of Mayoral Leadership	129
	A Hypothetical Contingency Theory of Mayoral Leadership	131
	Implications of a Contingency Theory for Mayoral Practice	137
	Racial Conflict and the American Mayor: Directions for Future Research	140
	Index	145
	About the Author	151

List of Tables and Figure

Tables

3-1   The Properties of Pluralized and Polarized Systems   38

7-1   Major Contextual, Power and Performance Dimensions
        of Mayoral Leadership in Cleveland, Gary, and Bir-
        mingham   110

7-2   Mayor-Council Cities of over 50,000 with more than 35
        percent of Population Black   118

Figure

8-1   A Contingency Model of Effective Mayoral Leadership   136

Preface

Research for this book began in response to a conversation with Peter Rossi about the relative effectiveness of Mayors Richard Hatcher and Carl Stokes after their first year-and-a-half in office. Leadership research in Gary and Cleveland, two racially polarized communities, posed a number of conceptual problems, because the research tradition surrounding mayoral behavior had always emphasized the pluralistic nature of urban politics. The popular media provided little help, since newspaper and television reporters tended to explain mayoral success and failure in terms of the personalities of individual mayors or cited the legal and financial constraints that limited mayoral influence. Even the comparative literature on racial conflict and polarization failed to provide answers to some of the questions my field research raised, because scholars of comparative political conflict tended to focus their attention on the macroaspects of divided societies, ignoring the role of political executives in mediating or exacerbating communal conflict. As my understanding of the political dynamics of mayoral leadership in Gary and Cleveland deepened, it became obvious that I would have to develop new models of mayoral leadership and clearer explanations of the impact of racial conflict on urban policy making.

This book is intended to add a new dimension to the study of American mayoral leadership. It argues that mayoral effectiveness is a joint product of contextual forces and purposeful choices; and that increased black political power over the past decade altered the nature of political forces in American cities, changing the strategic options available to mayors. To explicate these changes, an analytical framework is presented that assumes: (1) that American cities are governable, or amenable to mayoral leadership initiatives; (2) that there is more than "one best way" to govern cities; and (3) that people of varying abilities occupy mayorships.

In developing the framework used in this study, I eventually paired a conflict perspective with the more traditional pluralist approach to studying urban politics, allowing for the inclusion of dimensions of urban politics not highlighted in earlier studies. This approach made clearer to me the implications of racial conflict patterns for mayoral recruitment, performance, and effectiveness in the three cities studied for this project. Because the framework is intended to be comparative, it will prove useful, I hope, when applied to the politics of other cities and other time periods.

This book is divided into four parts. Part I introduces the study. Part II critically evaluates the generalizability of the pluralist model of mayoral leadership and presents alternative models of mayoral leadership for racially polarized contexts. Part III presents impressionistic case studies of Cleveland, Gary, and Birmingham—three racially polarized communities—to illustrate the impact of racial polarization on mayoral leadership. Part IV concludes the book, summarizing the case studies to support the argument, discussing the future of the American mayoralty, and presenting a sketch of a contingency theory of mayoral effectiveness.

I have written this book with the intent of presenting something new in urban political analysis. As such, it presents some unpopular ideas. I hope the reader will bear with me to the end, join the argument, and contribute something of his own to the underveloped science of urban leadership.

A number of kind friends contributed time, resources, ideas, and encouragement to this project. York Willbern directed my first efforts to struggle with this problem at Indiana University. While he may not agree with this resolution of it, he has been supportive throughout our association. Clifford Kaufman encouraged me to consult the literature on comparative politics for answers to some nagging theoretical problems and provided friendship and support throughout the writing of this book. Thomas Murphy introduced me to the patient people at Lexington Books, and James Carroll and Robert Iversen provided much appreciated resources and backup support. Throughout this project, Robert Backoff provided theoretical guidance and friendship. Others who read and criticized parts of what eventually became this book are: Charles Hyneman, William Siffin, Alfred Diamant, Richard Farmer, Harlan Hahn, E. Lester Levine, James Perry, Jeffrey Pressman, Clarence Stone, R. William Holland, Robert Whelan, Frederick Thayer, Dwight Waldo, Lloyd Nigro, and Michael White. In their own way, each helped to create an environment in which fragments of ideas were able to develop into integrated arguments. Their help and criticism was appreciated, even if I did not always heed their advice.

In Gary, Cleveland, and Birmingham, a number of busy city officials and community leaders, too numerous to mention individually, took time out to give valuable information and guidance. Their help is gratefully appreciated.

I would also like to express my appreciation to René Pavlock, who typed the manuscript and prodded me to meet numerous deadlines.

My wife, Elaine, must share much of the credit for the completion of this book. She lived in Gary and Cleveland in the summer of 1969, helped in the interviewing, arranged logistics, typed, and proofread. Just as important, she tolerated my periods of frustration, depression, anxiety, and occasional euphoria.

**Part I
Introduction**

1 Racial Conflict and the Paradox of Mayoral Leadership

Rioting in America's black ghettos in the mid-sixties brought to the nation's attention the implications of the "urban crisis" for the political stability of our major cities. The rioting exposed the physical and communal deterioration of America's central cities, and investigations into the causes of the rioting revealed that our cities are increasingly being populated by a bitter, ghettoized black underclass with serious economic, social, physical, and psychic deprivations. The Kerner Commission explicated a number of these urban and race relations problems and recommended programs that different levels of government could implement to alleviate the causes of the rioting.[1] At the local level, the commission expressed disappointment at the behavior of big city mayors; many had failed to provide the statesmanship necessary to mobilize their communities in campaigns to attack many obvious ghetto maladies. To improve local leadership, the commission outlined its model of ideal mayoral leadership:

Now, as never before, the American city has need for the personal qualities of strong democratic leadership. Given the difficulties and delays involved in administrative reorganization or institutional change, the best hope for the city in the short run lies in this powerful instrument. In most cities, the mayor will have the prime responsibility.

It is in large part his role now to create a sense of commitment and concern for the problems of the ghetto community and to set the tone for the entire relationship between the institutions of city government and all the citizenry.

Part of the task is to interpret the problems of the ghetto community to the citizenry at large and to generate channels of communication between Negro and white leadership outside of government. Only if all the institutions of the community—those outside of government as well as those inside the structure—are implicated in the problems of the ghetto, can the alienation and distrust of disadvantaged citizens be overcome.

This is now the decisive role for the urban mayor. As leader and mediator, he must involve all those groups—employers, news media, unions, financial institutions and others—which only together can bridge the chasm now separating the racial ghetto from the community. His goal, in effect, must be to develop a new working concept of democracy within the city.[2]

The urgent tone of this model implies that the office of mayor is occupied by unqualified timeservers and the office itself limited to ceremonial powers. Since the 1930s, however, a number of truly outstanding people have been elected to the mayorships of large cities, and many cities have strengthened the powers of the office of mayor.[3] In many of the cities where

3

rioting occurred the mayoralty was occupied by men of wide experience, energy, and considerable talent. The contradiction between the criticisms and prescriptions of the Kerner Commission and the quality of mayors presents a paradox: Why were the highly qualified mayors of riot-torn cities unable to provide the kind of leadership the commission prescribed?

The answer lies in the liberal nature of the Kerner Commission's recommendations.[4] In its approach to improving mayoral leadership, the commission sought mayors who would persuade community elites to support programs that would improve the conditions of ghetto life and that would, in turn, benefit the whole community. But, even in those communities where powerful institutions like banks, media, and manufacturing concerns were committed to changing ghetto living conditions (at least to the point where the danger of rioting would be minimized), mayors were often unsympathetic to programs that promised to antagonize their white constituents. During the late 1960s, a number of white liberal mayors who received extensive federal funds and favorable national publicity for programs aimed at improving ghetto conditions were soundly defeated for reelection alerting other mayors to the hazards of promoting ghetto development. Obviously, the Kerner Commission's model for ideal mayoral leadership had some major shortcomings when translated to the real world of urban politics.

A number of attempts were made to explain the demise of white liberal mayors, the rise and success of white "law and order" candidates, and the emergence of black mayors and mayoral candidates.[5] The near impossibility of simultaneously attempting to meet the needs of blacks and the demands of white constituents figured prominently in these explanations. The white liberal mayor of the late sixties was caught in a conflict of expectations between blacks and white liberals on one side demanding that he devote greater attention to meeting the needs of blacks; and on the other side, a resentful white central-city constituency insisting on lower taxes, more police protection, and restraints on housing, school, and employment integration. To compound these debilitating counterpressures, mayors were confronted by restive and independent bureaucracies and city councils, weakening the mayoralty and creating mayors reluctant to promote innovations that might cause greater disharmony and end their political careers.

The inherent instability of this situation helps to explain why the Kerner Commission's plea for aggressive mayoral leadership came at a time when outstanding people were occupying mayorships. The deep division between the kind of leadership the Kerner Commission prescribed to attack urban problems and the behavior white electorates would support produced mayoral caution except in those cities where mayors would risk their political futures.

The 1960s marked the rise of black political power in American cities. Protests, both violent and nonviolent, over discriminatory practices in government, housing, and employment produced concessions, but did not substantially change patterns of alienation, residence, or income. Limited housing and employment opportunities caused the accumulation and concentration of large blocs of black inner city voters, creating substantial black political power in local elections, forcing open local decision-making agendas, and causing the politics of a number of cities to shift from pluralized patterns of multilateral competition to polarized patterns of bipolar conflict. For mayors, black and white, community conflict rooted in racial disharmony meant frustration and political paralysis. But for some it also offered an opportunity—a chance to rise from political obscurity by championing the cause of their race.

Objectives

The study of mayoral leadership has been approached from a number of different perspectives and methodologies.[6] Unfortunately, little attention has been given in these research efforts to how variations in major contextual factors affect patterns of leadership style, structure, strategy, and performance. Curiously, most urban studies concerned with the political consequences of executive leadership have been in communities characterized by political pluralism and low or moderate degrees of conflict.[7] In these studies there has been considerable interest in the methods used by executives to promote the political integration of diverse community interests, leading analysts to equate effective leadership with a mayor's ability to create an integrative "convergence of power" by building an "executive-centered coalition."

But, one of the major contextual factors in an executive's political environment—the extent of community cleavage—has not been considered an important variable in most studies of mayoral leadership. Clearly, increases in black urban populations have combined with rising black militancy, the specter of ghetto rioting, and the uneasiness and hostility of white working-class residents of the central city to produce racial cleavages far more severe than the cleavage patterns found in the cities studied in earlier analyses of mayoral leadership.[8] Yet the commonly accepted "model" or major perspective on mayoral leadership is based mainly on research in communities interpreted in the literature as pluralistic. While a number of scholars have explained the biases of pluralist analysis and have noted the variable nature of community power and conflict structures, the inherent bias of leadership models predicated on pluralist interpretations of urban politics has been overlooked.[9] By basing their analyses of mayoral performance on the pluralist leadership framework and underemphasizing the variable nature of community conflict structures across communities, political analysts have overlooked an important constraint on mayoral leadership and may have overestimated the potential of mayors, no matter what the personality, skills, or institutional resources of the individual, to accomplish major change in many American cities.

The major thrust of this book is the analysis of mayoral leadership in racially cleaved communities. Limitations in the literature on mayoral leadership raise several questions considered:

1. What forms of mayoral leadership can be identified? Mainly, the literature focuses on the strategy of building an "executive-centered coalition" through the integration of diverse community interests.

2. Under what conditions is an "executive-centered coalition" an appropriate and effective strategy for mayoral leadership? This book argues partly that its effectiveness is limited to, and has been evaluated only in, communities with low or moderate cleavages.

3. In high-cleavage communities, what models of mayoral leadership are appropriate for analysis and effective in practice? Because there is little research on mayoral leadership in such communities and there is reason to question the universal applicability of pluralist models, this study develops alternative models of mayoral leadership for polarized communities and uses them to understand politics in Gary, Cleveland, and Birmingham, where mayors have served under conditions of intense racial hostility.

Besides these major questions, other, less central issues are also considered:

1. What changes occur in a city when a mayor is elected under the widely shared expectation that he will function as a "change agent" once in office?

2. What constraints in American cities shape the feasibility of alternate courses of leadership behavior?

3. How do these constraints influence leadership styles, strategies, structures, goals, and performances?

4. What tentative conclusions can be drawn about the style of mayoral leadership that will have the "best fit" in particular contexts?

Methodology

This book uses case studies of three American mayors to explore the impact of racial cleavage patterns on mayoral recruitment, behavior, and effectiveness. In addition, institutional and power structure configurations are also considered to have important independent influences on mayoral role playing. While this book focuses on the structural, institutional, and demographic properties of cities to explain most of the variance in mayoral achievement, there can be no doubt that the personality, ambition, and attitudes of individual mayors affect their performance. Therefore, psychological factors will be considered when they are an obvious aid in understanding relevant mayoral behavior.

Each of the three case studies presented represents a type of mayoral performance. Because the cases were selected to illustrate rather than to systematically test propositions, their uniqueness limits the generalizability of the findings. Nevertheless, a number of propositions can be drawn from these cases that can be suggestive guideposts for future studies of mayoral leadership and urban politics. Their presentation conforms in different ways to what Lijphart calls "hypothesis-generating case studies," "theory-confirming case studies," "theory-infirming case studies," and "deviant case studies."[10] They are used to generate, confirm, reject, modify, and limit propositions about mayoral leadership.

The case study method has some well known and obvious limitations. Most of the criticisms of case studies have focused upon either their dramatic tone, research procedures, or social-scientific relevance.[11] While critics concede that case studies are suggestive and educational, they fault them for being impressionistic and not suited to the systematic generation of propositions; because cases tend to stress the dramatic, the pathological, and the deviant, they rarely use, or are useful in, comparative inquiry.

The case study, however, can be quite a useful method if these criticisms are taken into account when designing a study and reporting findings. Available research methods can be built into case studies in a number of ways. For example, cases can be assembled in a comparative framework; they can be related to the existing literature, and they can use a common unit of analysis, common hypotheses,[12] or conceptual schemes to place cases into common perspectives.[13]

In the three case studies presented in this book, efforts have been made to conform to techniques designed to add theoretical import to case studies. The cases support the general proposition that mayoral leadership initiatives are conditioned by community conflict patterns.

The following chapter presents a detailed review of the literature on mayoral leadership in pluralist systems. This discussion provides a background for a critique of the pluralist leadership model and for the examination of the influence of racial conflict on mayoral leadership presented in chapter 3. The case studies follow in chapters 4 through 6. Finally, chapters 7 and 8 review findings from the three cases and discuss the implications of racial conflict for mayoral leadership and leadership research in the future.

Notes

1. See National Advisory Commission on Civil Disorders, *Report* (Washington, D.C.: Government Printing Office, 1967), hereinafter cited as *"Kerner Report."*

2. Ibid., p. 155.

3. See Seymour Freedgood, "New Strength in City Hall," in the Editors of *Fortune, The Exploding Metropolis* (Garden City, N.Y.: Doubleday & Co., 1958), pp. 62-91.

4. See Norval D. Glenn, "The Kerner Report, Social Scientists and the American Public: Introduction to a Symposium," *Social Science Quarterly* 49 (December 1968), pp. 433-37.

5. See, for example: James Q. Wilson and Harold Wilde, "The Urban Mood," *Commentary* 48 (October 1969), pp. 52-61; Fred Powledge, "The Flight from City Hall," *Harper's Magazine* 239 (November 1969), pp. 69-86; and James Q. Wilson, "The Mayors vs. the Cities," *Public Interest* 16 (Summer 1969), pp. 25-37.

6. For a reasonably comprehensive listing of the varied approaches to studying political leadership, see Glenn D. Paige, ed. *Political Leadership: Readings for an Emerging Field* (New York: Macmillan Co., Free Press, 1972), pp. 8-9.

7. Chapter 2 reviews this literature in greater depth.

8. The Kerner Commission noted the nature of change in urban conflict patterns and extensively discussed the critical role of mayors in mediating racial conflict. Interestingly, the commission failed to discuss the constraints racial conflict imposed on mayors already committed to biracial leadership. See the *Kerner Report,* pp. 285-99.

9. See, for examples: William E. Connolly, ed. *The Bias of Pluralism* (New York: Atherton Press, 1969); Charles A. McCoy and John Playford, eds. *Apolitical Politics: A Critique of Behavioralism* (New York: Thomas Y. Crowell Co., 1967); and Peter Bachrach and Morton S. Baratz, *Power and Poverty* (New York: Oxford University Press, 1970).

10. Arend Lijphart, "Comparative Politics and the Comparative Method," *American Political Science Review* 65 (September 1971), pp. 682-93.

11. See Morris Davis and Marvin G. Weinbaum, *Metropolitan Decision Processes* (Chicago: Rand McNally & Co., 1969), p. 4.

12. See James E. Jernberg, "On Taking the Next Step in Case Studies," *Public Administration Review* 29 (July-August 1969), pp. 410-17.

13. See Michael Haas and Theodore Becker, "A Multimethodological Plea," *Polity* 2 (Spring 1970), p. 284.

Part II
Racial Conflict and Models
of Mayoral Leadership

2

The Pluralist Model of Mayoral Leadership: An Overgeneralized Strategy for Limited Contexts

During the past decade, city politics have become a major focus of political inquiry after many years of academic neglect.[1] Most studies of urban politics have focused on specific policy problems or community decision making. Only a few studies have carefully examined the role of a single actor, interest group, or policy-making body in a systematic comparative manner.[2] Until 1970, with a few notable exceptions, the study of mayoral leadership was neglected by political scientists, except for occasional discussions of mayoral influence in policy controversies like flouridation, urban renewal, school integration, and metropolitan consolidation.[3]

The four most notable exceptions to the general neglect of the urban mayor during the 1960s, Dahl's *Who Governs?*,[4] Banfield's *Political Influence*,[5] Lowi's *At the Pleasure of the Mayor*,[6] and Sayre and Kaufman's *Governing New York City*,[7] had significant impact on the discipline of political science and subsequent research on mayoral leadership. When these studies are combined with the numerous atheoretical case histories and autobiographies of big city mayors written during the 1950s and 1960s,[8] a wealth of suggestive material becomes available to generate explanatory, evaluative, and strategic models for mayoral leadership.

In recent years, a number of authors have used comparative approaches to advance theory building about mayoral leadership. Cunningham's *Urban Leadership in the Sixties*,[9] Roger's *The Management of Big Cities*,[10] and articles by George,[11] Greenstone and Peterson,[12] Salisbury,[13] and Kotter and Lawrence [14] have advanced our knowledge about the tactics and constraints that enhance or limit mayoral effectiveness. Together, the earlier studies of mayoral leadership and the more recent additions have produced a framework that has been accepted as a paradigm for the study of mayoral leadership.[15] These efforts have resulted in the accumulation of a body of propositions on the verge of forming a middle-range theory of mayoral leadership.[16] However, the universal applicability of the dominant model of mayoral leadership is unfortunately limited by the composition of the sample of cities studied, the individualistic bias of some analysts, and the integrationist and order biases of some interpretations. To become an empirically useful model, a leadership construct must either apply to all situations or specify its limits.[17] The dominant model of mayoral leadership developed during the 1960s fails to meet these criteria because it has failed to account for the importance of community conflict

11

on mayoral performance and has proposed a model of leadership effectiveness that is contingent on pluralistic contexts. Despite these limitations, the dominant model does apply to numerous situations and provides a useful inventory of concepts to construct alternative models for contexts where its major variables take on different weights.

Mayoral Leadership as a Problem of Methodology

The concept of "leadership" poses many operational difficulties. It has been used in so many different ways to characterize diverse phenomena that its usefulness as a social science concept has been seriously questioned.[18] Many of the problems with the concept stem from its origins as a commonplace term that communicates general meaning but hardly lends itself to rigorous scientific investigation.[19] While these conceptional difficulties and methodological controversies have caused confusion and retarded the development of theories of political leadership, there has emerged, nevertheless, a widely shared view that "effective leadership" should be associated with the attainment of goals and the exercise of influence.[20]

Over the past forty years, leadership has been studied from a number of different perspectives, disciplinary approaches, varied contexts, and levels of analysis.[21] There has been so little agreement about the phenomena studied or the proper use of the concept that Warren Bennis has observed:

Of all the hazy and confounding areas in social psychology, leadership theory undoubtedly contends for top nomination. And ironically, probably more has been written and less is known about leadership than about any other topic in the behavioral sciences. . . . So we have invented an endless proliferation of terms to deal with it: leadership, power, status, authority, rank, prestige, influence, control, manipulation, domination, and so forth, and still the concept is not sufficiently defined. As we survey the path leadership theory has taken, we spot the wreckage of "trait theory," the "great man" theory, the "situationalist critique," leadership styles, functional leadership, and finally, leaderless leadership; to say nothing of bureaucratic leadership, charismatic leadership, democratic-autocratic-laissez-faire leadership, group-centered leadership, reality-centered leadership, leadership by objective, and so on. The dialectic and reversals of emphases in this area very nearly rival the tortuous twists and turns of child-rearing practices.[22]

The field of political science has experienced many of these same conceptual problems, causing considerable confusion, much methodological debate, and little advancement of leadership theory itself.[23] Recently, many political scientists have begun to focus their research on leadership preformance, "what leaders do and how they do it."[24] Edinger's definition of "leadership" serves as a useful summary of the performance orientation. It emphasizes goal-directed and influence-wielding aspects of political leadership and allows for the integration of a number of levels of analysis, additional concepts, and alternative styles, resources, strategies, and contexts:

Leadership is seen as the ability to guide and structure the collective behavior patterns of a given group in a desired direction, so that the decisions of the leader are implemented by group action. The leader is followed because he is loved, admired, respected, or feared, because he can coerce, persuade, or manipulate group members, because he can offer psychic as well as material rewards and punishments, or because compliance with his wishes is sanctioned by habit, traditional or legal-rational behavior norms.[25]

Within this definition, concepts such as power, decision making, control, conflict, and exchange can be brought into a leadership analysis simply by adding to Edinger's framework. The approach can accommodate concerns with leadership in the context of interpersonal interactions, small groups, formal organizations, communities, and social movements. More importantly, the performance approach can be used to differentiate between leadership styles, identify salient preconditions, develop standards of effectiveness, and determine ''best fit'' strategies for particular types of contexts.

The performance approach to leadership analysis stresses goal attainment and, in a governmental setting, policy output. But focusing exclusively on policy output has serious pitfalls. Policy outputs and impacts are difficult to identify and measure; they often have long-term and overlapping spillover effects that cannot easily be understood or predicted.[26] A mayor's operative goals are difficult to specify, because separating symbolic from substantive goals can be an elusive undertaking.[27] Most mayors have many goals, and the multidimensional nature of performance criteria often produces claims of satisfactory performance when only one of many dimensions of achievement have been met. Nondecision making can also be a performance goal and presents a complex theoretical and operational problem for the leadership analyst.[28] Despite these problems, it is still possible to use goals and policy outputs as measures of leadership effectiveness, provided the criteria is multidimensional and includes a variety of politically relevant variables.[29]

An alternative to focusing exclusively on policy outputs in evaluating leadership effectiveness is to evaluate the preconditions necessary for mayoral leadership, those styles, goals, resources, and environments most likely to aid or constrain mayoral goal attainment. Because students of mayoral behavior have linked mayors' styles,[30] goals, resources,[31] and leadership structures[32] to outputs in both explicit and implicit ways, we have been provided with valuable ''secondary criteria'' for evaluating performance.[33] These preconditions serve as valuable aids to analysis as long as the distinction between necessary and sufficient conditions is kept in mind.[34]

The use of styles, goals, resources, and structures is also justifiable on other grounds. The evaluation of a mayor's leadership ability must extend beyond his achievements in a short time frame. An evaluation must also include the mayor's capability for structuring other actor's expectations and predispositions for compliance and cooperation so that future proposals and programs will be readily supported and implemented. These features of mayoral leadership constitute a relatively persistent structure of influence that transcends short time frames.

The Dominant Model of Mayoral Effectiveness

The dominant model of mayoral effectiveness incorporates a number of models that have evolved since the 1920s. It consists of elements of more or less complete models that may be called the "business management model," the "entrepreneur model," the "political broker model," the "great man model," the "resources model," the "high energy" or "activist model," and the "network model."[35] Each of these models is somewhat at odds with the others, offering different explanations and tactics for mayoral success and failure. Nevertheless, their differences are reconcilable and their principal components may be integrated into a conceptual scheme even though there are contradictions and inconsistencies in some parts of their logic. All these "submodels" share the common view that leadership is in some sense a structure of influence.

Mayoral Leadership as a Structure of Influence

In bits and pieces and sometimes in more general statements, the major features of a theory of mayoral leadership have been accumulating over the past four decades. Synthesizing the elements of this dominant paradigm requires that some features be more emphasized than others. Nevertheless, for the past few years there has been a good deal of consensus among students of mayoral behavior that the appropriate approach to mayoral leadership should analyze elements of entrepreneurship, coalition formation, resources, and goals.

A common theme in the literature is the distinction between headship and leadership.[36] The former involves merely occupying an elective or appointive position, while the latter involves the exercising of influence in the pursuit of goals. Implementing innovations by successfully expanding formal authority through the exercise of informal influence frequently has been interpreted in terms of political integration and coalition formation and has often been considered a measure of effective executive performance.[37]

The performance perspective views leadership as an entrepreneurial task. To be feasible, every goal, program, and policy requires that a set of powers and resources be mobilized and committed to it. These powers and resources are normally dispersed in a community among several semi-independent elites. Stinchcombe observes: "The problem of entre-preneurship is to assemble these powers and commit them to the project. Assembly involves on the one hand negotiation with the elites who hold the powers and on the other the modification of the proposal until its power requirements can be assembled."[38] The extent to which the relevant elites are favorably predisposed to welcome proposals from the entrepreneur (mayor) determines the scope of his policy alternatives. From this set of alternatives, a mayor may choose a course of action with a minimum risk of failure. However, if he wishes to promote a program involving powers and resources not contained in the sympathetic or controlled parts of his leadership structure or network, he must bargain, negotiate, and persuade through exchange relationships with those elites who control requisite resources. The configuration of a leader's interorganizational and interpersonal network, including policy arenas, relevant elites, their interests and relationships, and the resources they control, comprise a leadership structure. It is a relatively persistent pattern of relationships, including both allies and enemies. If a leader confronts a situation where he cannot implement a program he values, he can scale down his goals or attempt to reshape the configuration of power and resources in his network so that the resources he needs will be controlled by people sympathetic to his goals.[39]

The entrepreneurial perspective on leadership views the effective mayor as capable of building broad feasibility sets within constraints imposed by the financial, administrative, technical, legal, and political power of counteractors. For the urban mayor, entrepreneurial behavior requires that he use his resources—personal, political, and institutional—with maximum efficiency to expand his feasibility sets to improve the probabilities for the successful implementation of his policy preferences and to decrease the feasibility of proposals he opposes. By increasing his feasibility set and building and maintaining the support of elements in his leadership network, the mayor-leader-entrepreneur sets the stage for the implementation of policies to create change in his city. Of course, a mayor still retains the choice whether to promote innovations or not, and his choice may be to use his power to retain the status quo by marshaling opposition to proposals for change.

This simple and brief description of mayoral leadership encompasses most of the factors that previous studies argue are significant for understanding mayoral effectiveness. It does not, however, sufficiently explicate major concepts or differentiate between types of mayoral performance. To better understand problems of mayoral leadership, it is appropriate first to distinguish between major types of leadership performance.

Mayoral Leadership as Civic Entrepreneurship,
Brokership, and Figureheadship

Three types of mayoral leadership styles can be identified in the literature on mayoral behavior: the civic entrepreneur, the broker, and the figurehead.[40] In spite of the many conceptual difficulties associated with the concept of "leadership," in pluralist analysis, leadership success is equated with entrepreneurial behavior;[41] the greater the entrepreneurial success, the more effective the leader.[42]

In pluralist systems, by definition, political power and resources —popular support, economic resources, administrative authority, and technical skills—are dispersed among several elites.[43] Almost any major innovation requires the mobilization of resources controlled by a number of different and often competing groups. The civic entrepreneur's problem is to build a centrally directed coalition that mobilizes and incorporates those groups who control the resources to make innovations feasible.[44] Thus, the civic entrepreneur has been defined by his high scores on such personality traits as originality, risk taking, initiative energy, openness, organizational ability, and promotional ingenuity.[45] Dahl's description of Mayor Lee's efforts in New Haven serves as an inventory of the dynamics of interpersonal relations as a mayor attempts to mobilize and focus diverse community interests.

It would be grossly misleading to see the executive-centered order as a neatly hierarchical system with the mayor at the top operating through subordinates in a chain of command. The mayor was not at the peak of a pyramid but rather at the center of intersecting circles. He rarely commanded. He negotiated, cajoled, insisted, demanded, even threatened, but he most needed support and acquiescence from other leaders who simply could not be commanded. Because the mayor could not command, he had to bargain.[46]

In the earlier pluralist studies of mayoral leadership, effective leadership involved converting the focus of community politics from a system of multilateral competition to a system of mayor-dominated politics.[47] Mayoral performance was assessed on four criteria: the mayor's ability to *centralize* or focus community politics on the mayoralty; to *mobilize* community involvement, to *integrate* diverse interests; and to activate *innovative* programs.[48]

During the era of the urban political machine, decision making was centralized through the use of patronage and party discipline. But as party discipline and the importance of patronage declined in the postwar era, a new pattern of leadership emerged that allowed some mayors to centralize decision making and in some cases to activate substantial innovative programs. According to Salisbury, in this new infrastructure the mayor is an individual who has (1) sufficient mass appeal and/or organizational support to win election, (2) enough awareness of the complexity of urban problems to rely heavily on a professional staff for advice and counsel, and (3) the ability to negotiate successfully with the economic notables in the city to mobilize both public and private resources in efforts to solve core city economic and social problems.[49]

The model *civic entrepreneur* is an activist adept at accumulating a variety of resources and skillful in using them to pyramid and centralize power in a system otherwise characterized by the fragmentation of formal authority and political influence among individuals, groups, and institutions holding veto privileges in the policy-making process.[50] The variety of groups holding veto power over policy making in such specific areas as education, law enforcement, welfare, housing, and taxation is often sufficiently overwhelming to induce some mayors to become mere *figureheads*, eschewing any form of leadership and innovation.[51] Because of the dispersion of power and veto privileges, some mayors have served as *brokers* among the competing groups and have built coalitions to promote inoffensive programs and to dispense services to established interests.[52]

While innovation is possible in pluralistic communities, it tends to be the exception rather than the rule. The fragmentation of political power often forces a mayor to behave conservatively rather than innovatively. Generally, the system is more favorable to defenders of the status quo.[53] The search for feasible overarching programs that maintain the status quo in power relationships (usually couched in the rhetoric of collective goods) has often become the major entrepreneurial task in pluralist communities. As the primacy of coalition maintenance displaces program innovation, the spirit of civic entrepreneurship is often displaced by the pragmatics of political brokership.[54]

The pragmatics of coalition maintenance confront the mayor with difficult choices. If he maintains the current coalition arrangement, programs offensive to elements of his coalition need to be modified in scope and intent. The alternative is to reshape the configuration of power in the community in order to have critical resources controlled by people sympathetic to his programs.[55] Clearly, it is less costly and less risky to modify programs and maintain a winning coalition. Thus, innovation and risk taking are often supplanted in the mayor's value hierarchy by stability and predictability. In many pluralistic cities, the mayoralty becomes a reactive role to proposals initiated by representatives of major community interests, rather than an entrepreneurial role initiating broad-scale innovations.[56]

In order to analyze the strengths and weaknesses of the dominant model of mayoral leadership, it is useful to examine its major components; leadership styles, goals, resources, structures, and contexts. The typology of leadership performance demonstrated how clusters of these variables tend to combine to produce entrepreneurship, brokership, and figureheadship. When all these factors are maximized, an entrepreneurial executive-centered coalition is likely to emerge.

Leadership Styles

The manner in which an individual adapts to a role is called a "style." We know very little about why men behave the way they do in certain leader-ship roles and why some bundles of behavior, or "styles," work and others fail.[57] But, years of research have revealed that successful leadership is not associated with one narrow fixed set of personality and physical characteristics[58] and that leadership is a process shaped and screened by culture and role expectations, "two contexts that tend to regularize and standardize . . . political performances."[59]

The concept of "leadership style" has been given many different mean-ings by leadership theorists and remains among the most illusive terms in the literature. Barber's definition provides one of the more useful treat-ments of the concept:

"Style" . . . means a collection of habitual action patterns in meeting role demands. Viewed from outside, a man's style is the observed quality and character of his performance. Viewed from inside, it is a bundle of strategies for adopting, for protecting and enhancing self-esteem.[60]

A leadership style is clearly a bridge between the psychological charac-teristics of an individual and the sociological properties of a role. By far the most explicit statement of the properties of effective mayoral style is found in Cunningham's *Urban Leadership in the Sixties*. In his analysis of the mayors of Chicago, Pittsburgh, Cleveland, and New Haven in the 1960s, Cunningham minimized the contextual differences between the cities so that he could concentrate on entrepreneurship.[61] Using an impressionistic measure of performance, based on originality, risk-taking initiative, energy, openness, organizational ability, and promotional ingenuity, Cun-ningham rated Mayor Lee of New Haven as the most entrepreneurial of the four mayors, followed by Mayors Barr of Pittsburgh, Daley of Chicago, and Locher of Cleveland.[62] In Cunningham's analysis, risk taking and original-ity were the two most important marks of a political entrepreneur's style. In contrast, a nonentrepreneur is a mayor whose style reflects "caution, inflexibility, bureaucratic authoritarianism, physical inertness, heavy-handedness, and organizational confusion."[63]

Despite some limitations, Cunningham's analysis provides a useful inventory of the principal ingredients of mayoral entrepreneurship.[64] Yet, entrepreneurial qualities are only necessary, not sufficient, conditions for promoting innovations, centralizing authority, mobilizing community resources, and integrating diverse interests. An entrepreneurial style alone does not ensure successful mayoral leadership. A mayor's goals and resources are also factors that condition mayoral effectiveness.

Goals

The operative goals a mayor pursues depends on his personal preferences and his calculation of feasibility. The variety of innovative programs and ideas available to a mayor are almost boundless. For example, Pressman suggests the following list of goals for mayoral action:

effective and humane law enforcement; redevelopment linked to speedy relocation in decent housing of those displaced by redevelopment; expansion of a city's financial resources by increasing taxes or by attraction of new industry; improvement of educational quality and relationships between the schools and the community; construction of low cost public housing; generation of new jobs and creation of job-training and job placement programs. Besides these substantive goals, the ideal mayor would strive to maintain within the political system a process of constructive dialogue between diverse groups which would contribute to harmony in the city.[65]

Instead of these liberal goals, a mayor might also choose more conservative, segregationist, or divisive policies—or no specific goals at all. More important is a mayor's choice between policies that have collective or distributive outcomes. Collective goods are nondivisible public policies whose primary impact benefits the whole community.[66] In an urban setting, pollution abatement, mass transit, and personal safety are examples of collective goods. In the public choice literature, the numerous exchange activities of a leader to facilitate the creation of collective goods are often equated with entrepreneurship.[67]

Instead of promoting collective goods, a mayor might choose a distributive strategy; that is, to promote divisible public policies that can be distributed exclusively to a single group or individual. The traditional currency of urban politics—patronage, special favors, licenses, zoning exemptions, regulatory enforcement (or lack of enforcement), and recognition—typifies distributive goods. The model political broker uses private goods as his stock in trade to retain power and maintain loyalties.

The blend of collective and distributive goods a mayor adapts as his program is often difficult to discern. Proposals for distributive programs, like the Kerner Commission's call for the improvement of ghetto living conditions, are often disguised as collective goods. Also, subtle, unannounced changes in policy frequently occur without publicity, only to be discovered months later. Nevertheless, it is possible to analyze an administration's operative goals which have major effects on a mayor's popularity and scope of achievements.

Resources

In the pursuit of his goals, a mayor will have to coerce, compromise, and accommodate a number of diverse governmental and nongovernmental actors. These usually include the city council, local party leaders, city bureaucrats, business elites, union officials, the press, and county, state, and national officials, as well as the local citizenry. His success at gaining their cooperation depends on his goals and the personal, political, and institutional resources at his disposal. The more hostility counteractors hold toward a goal, the more resources a mayor will have to expend to overcome resistance and assure compliance.

In bargaining with other elites, the resources at the mayor's command are critically important and vary with the individual mayor and the political and institutional structure of the city. The mayor's entrepreneurial skills, charisma, and historical ties to other elites are resources that can be expended in exchanges to win support for his goals.[68] Institutional resources, like financial slack,[69] staff manpower, jurisdiction, appointing powers, patronage, veto power, an executive budget, and a partisan electoral system are also important.[70] Finally, media support, supportive interest groups, and a tradition of community mobilization behind mayor-directed programs are also valuable resources.

The extent to which normative resources like personal and community loyalties can be substituted for remunerative, divisible, and costly resources like patronage and personal favors affects a mayor's alternatives.[71] Under conditions of hostility and distrust, appeals to personal and community loyalties are devalued and must be augmented with expensive inducements to gain support for a mayor's progran, narrowing the scope of his feasibility set. Many mayoral leadership problems can be explained by the mayor's lack of requisite resources for the political climate in his community.

In the dominant model of mayoral leadership, an effective mayor promotes collective goods and is equipped with a wide range of resources to exchange for support. Without collective goods as goals, a mayor is reduced to brokership. Without resources, a mayor may be reduced to figureheadship.

Leadership Structures

The mayor and his staff function in a complex web of interorganizational and interpersonal relationships. Three dimensions of this structure are particularly important to understanding mayoral effectiveness: polarity, mode of bargaining, and interpersonal relations. In pluralized communities that are either nonpolar, unipolar, or multipolar; have a tradition of harmony, integration and constraint in conflicts; and where elites have engaged in a series of positive-sum bargains, coalitions, and exchanges, a mayor's leadership task will be considerably eased. On the other hand, bipolarity, conflict, fragmentation, and rancorousness in political conflict, combined with a tradition of zero-sum policy battles, minimize opportunities for mayoral leadership.[72]

The configuration of a community's decision-making structure is of great importance to the mayor, because it comprises: the number of influences in the community with which he must contend, the different kinds of political resources held by each counteractor, their relationships and relative power to one another, their area of special policy concern, their leadership and intraorganizational characteristics, their biases, their historical ties to the mayor and his staff, and the incentives to which they are likely to respond. No mayor's agenda will be universally acclaimed, and support may shift from issue to issue. Therefore, a mayor must constantly nurture his links with groups in his leadership structure and be on the alert for changes in relationships that might affect his structure of support. Likewise, an entrepreneurial mayor must constantly work to broaden his support among recalcitrant and emerging groups.[73]

A supportive community decision-making network is also an important precondition for innovative mayoral leadership. The mayor's definition of local problems and opportunities for change depends on the receptivity of other elites in his community. But, the politics of many cities are characterized by fragmentation, "baronial power-seeking," and dysfunctional political infighting.[74] To overcome the debilitating effects of political fragmentation and conflict, mayors must establish centralizing coalitions. If a network is properly integrated, centralized, and maintained and has the requisite powers to implement reforms, a mayor can expect to have few problems implementing new programs. Naturally, change is never simply a process of command, but the task is relatively easy compared to the problems of promoting new programs in a hostile decision-making environment.

The Limits Of Mayoral Leadership

Even if a mayor is endowed with all the necessary preconditions (appropriate style, goals, resources, and decision-making structure), there is no guarantee that he will be an effective leader because the model of mayoral leadership that has dominated political analysis was developed in and is only applicable to pluralized systems. In earlier studies, mayoral performance was evaluated against a single standard—the executive-centered coalition—and within a single context—pluralized systems—ignoring the influence of different configurations of community conflict on leadership strategies. Thus, pluralist analysis

has greater applicability to homogeneous societies, characterized by pluralism, fundamental sociopolitical agreement, limited conflict, and consensus about the fundamental nature of politics and government, and in which most political decisions are routine, specific choices concerning incremental changes in governmental policies.[75]

In pluralistic systems, leaders face conflicting claims and demands for role performance and must adopt a variety of methods to reduce role conflict.[76] Leaders resolve role conflict by evoking socially approved strategies for noncompliance,[77] withdrawing,[78] or redefining the situation by developing overarching programs that can be used to mediate conflicting expectations.[79] McFarland observes:

In a pluralistic society, the institutionalized mediator with an autonomous range of power can be a certain type of politician who is sensitive to multilateral conflict and accordingly redefines particular, limited situations to resolve conflict, satisfy the majority of conflicting interests involved, and enhance his own popularity.[80]

To support this argument, McFarland cites the case of New Haven's Mayor Lee and his urban renewal program, which he calls "a creative, if limited redefinition of the situation in terms of upgrading common interests."[81]

It is important to notice that McFarland states that the leadership pattern he calls "dynamic mediation" refers to limited situations and multilateral conflict. If, however, major changes are called for, beyond "limited redefinition of the situation," and the conflict pattern in a community is more bipolar than multipolar, the leadership structure preferred by advocates of "executive-centered coalitions" may be both impossible to bring about and undesirable as a strategic means to social change.

Racial Polarization as a Constraint on Mayoral Leadership

In every community there is some conflict associated with the management of local government. However, the structure of conflict—its participants, stakes, intensity, focus, and forms of expression—differ across communities and over time. Studies of mayoral behavior have given too little attention to these variations and their effect on leadership style, strategy, and performance. Since political structures vary, the pluralist model of mayoral leadership must be only one of a potential set of models of mayoral behavior. Its value as an explanatory tool, a strategic device, or an evaluative standard depends on its fit with a complex, variegated reality.[82] How well does the pluralist leadership model fit contemporary urban realities?

In many American cities racial polarization has produced racial conflict far more severe than the conflict discussed in earlier studies of mayoral leadership. The political structure of many cities has changed from a system of multipolar competition of a low or moderate intensity to a system of bipolar or polarized conflict. Under conditions of racial polarization, both black and white leaders seek to block new policies that benefit the other racial group.[83] The obstructionist tactics of racial politics help to explain the political immobilism in many American cities and the demise of innovation-minded mayors.

Three of the structural preconditions that underpin pluralist politics are worth examining in the context of racial polarization: (1) an expanding set of divisible political stakes and collective goods that can be allocated without emotionally charged aftereffects; (2) fundamental sociopolitical agreement among a substantial majority of citizens; and (3) a commitment by officials and interest group leaders to a set of rules or bargaining conventions that lends stability and legitimacy to the policy-making process.[84] As many American cities entered the last half of the 1960s, a change occurred in each of these preconditions mitigating against the successful application of pluralist politics and consequently mayoral entrepreneurship.

Even the casual observer notices the increased scarcity, in most major cities, of those substantive stakes usually associated with urban politics: public office or employment, money, and government services.[85] Even when some slack resources can be found or when symbolic rewards can be substituted for substantive programs, mutual suspicion between white and black leaders often makes any form of brokering or innovation impossible.[86] Under conditions of racial polarization, issues that might be considered public or collective goods and that conform to the model of the overarching policy (urban renewal, pollution control, recreation programs, and law and order policies) are often interpreted by their distributional impacts, favoring one racial group at the expense of the other.[87] In communities beset by racial polarization, "communitywide" programs are interpreted in terms of their secondary impacts and in terms of their symbolic significance.[88] Even broker-oriented coalitions are extremely difficult to assemble, because racial group leaders are continually on their guard against the threat of co-optation.[89]

In short, under conditions of racial polarization: (1) programs are interpreted for their psychic effects on the self-image of the contesting groups;

(2) the distributional impacts of new proposals come under close scrutiny; (3) proposals are evaluated for their opportunity costs (what other program might better benefit either the black or white communities?);[90] and (4) the long-run political consequences of an innovation are carefully analyzed (will a new program ultimately strengthen one side at the expense of the other?).

Indeed, until recently, the political manifestations of racial polarization were submerged beneath the surface of urban politics by a number of devices, such as racial balancing of candidate slates by local political parties, the structuring of electoral rules to diminish black electoral strength, and the willingness of some black politicians to "go along" with local white leadership because they personally profited by the arrangement or were afraid they would lose whatever little influence they had if they "kicked up a fuss."[91] During the early civil-rights period of the late 1950s and early 1960s, race issues were rarely articulated in urban policy-making councils. In the period following the Watts rioting, aspiring politicians of both races have exploited racial antagonisms to mobilize solid blocs of voting support and build community organizations. A number have chosen to make racial issues a dominant part of their political style to further their political careers. Fundamental sociopolitical agreement and commitment to the rules and conventions of political competition dissipate as the incentives of political opportunity and racial mobilization favor rancorous conflict behavior. Under these conditions, there is a mutual escalation of racial polarization, racial consciousness, and subsequently—immobilism. Innovation in both distributive and collective goods suffers.[92] For the innovation-minded mayor, only frustration can result.

The constraints on mayoral leadership caused by racial polarization are rooted in the social structure of American cities. It is unreasonable to expect a leadership structure, such as an executive-centered coalition, that is appropriate and effective in one context (in this case, pluralist systems) to be feasible in all contexts. By failing to differentiate between contexts and implicitly assuming a pluralist environment, the literature on mayoral leadership has tended to promote one model of mayoral leadership as preferable for *all* communities: the executive-centered coalition. Mayors have been ranked, explicitly or implicitly, on a scale that assumes the conflict patterns of all communities are similar and that similar strategies should be equally effective.[93] The only variables in this form of analysis are the resources of the mayor and the entrepreneurial ability of the person occupying the mayoral role.

In summary, by basing their interpretive model or strategy on the pluralist leadership framework and underemphasizing the variable nature of community conflict structures, political scientists, mayors, and citizens may overestimate the potential of a mayor—no matter what his personality, skills, or institutional resources—to be an effective civic entrepreneur. Further, the bias of pluralism may lead a student of mayoral behavior to ignore other effective leadership strategies and the contributions of those mayors who cannot or do not choose to be entrepreneurs in the pluralist sense. It may also mislead well-meaning mayors to pursue strategies that are unproductive or self-defeating. Finally, by using a rarely attained model—the civic entrepreneur—as an evaluative standard, critics might be too harsh on individual mayors and too hopeful that someone else can be more effective in their communities.

Notes

1. See Lawrence J.R. Herson, "The Lost World of Municipal Government," *American Political Science Review* 51 (June 1957), pp. 330-45; and Robert T. Daland, "Political Science and the Study of Urbanism," *American Political Science Review* 51 (June 1957), pp. 491-509.

2. Many of these earlier studies are referred to in Edward C. Banfield and James Q. Wilson, *City Politics* (Cambridge, Mass.: Harvard University Press, 1963), especially section IV, "Some Political Roles." More recent studies have been discussed by Robert L. Lineberry and Ira Sharkansky, in *Urban Politics and Public Policy* (New York: Harper & Row, 1971), in chapter 5, "Decision-Making in Urban Government." The "bay area" study conducted by Heinz Eulau and his students is probably the most comprehensive comparative examination of a single urban institution, the city council, ever undertaken. See Heinz Eulau and Kenneth Prewitt, *Labyrinths of Democracy: Adaptions, Linkages, Representation, and Policies in Urban Politics* (Indianapolis: Bobbs-Merrill Co., 1973).

3. See Robert L. Crain, Elihu Katz, and Donald B. Rosenthal, *The Politics of Community Conflict: The Flouridation Decision* (Indianapolis: Bobbs-Merrill Co., 1969); Amos H. Hawley, "Community Power and Urban Renewal Success," *American Journal of Sociology* 68 (January 1963), pp. 422-51; Robert L. Crain, *The Politics of School Desegregation* (Chicago: Aldine-Atherton, 1968); and for an excellent collection of excerpts from studies dealing with the politics of metropolitan reorganization, see Michael N. Danielson, ed. *Metropolitan Politics: A Reader* (Boston: Little, Brown & Co., 1966).

4. Robert A. Dahl, *Who Governs?: Democracy and Power in an American City* (New Haven: Yale University Press, 1961).

5. Edward C. Banfield, *Political Influence* (New York: The Free Press, 1961).

6. Theodore J. Lowi, *At the Pleasure of the Mayor,* (New York: The Free Press, 1964).

7. Wallace S. Sayre and Herbert Kaufman, *Governing New York City: Politics in the Metropolis* (New York: W.W. Norton & Co., 1965).

8. Among the more noteworthy or these efforts are: Walton Bean, *Boss Ruef's San Francisco* (Berkeley: University of California Press, 1952); William F. Buckley, Jr. *The Unmaking of a Mayor* (New York: Viking Press, 1966); Barbara Carter, *The Road to City Hall: How John V. Lindsay Became Mayor* (Englewood Cliffs, N.J.: Prentice-Hall, 1967); James M. Curley, *I'd Do It Again* (Englewood Cliffs, N.J.: Prentice-Hall, 1957); Gene Fowler, *Beau James: The Life and Times of Jimmy Walker* (New York: Viking Press, 1949); Charles Garrett, *The La Guardia Years: Machine and Reform Politics in New York City* (New Brunswick, N.J.: Rutgers University Press, 1961); Alex Gottfried, *Boss Cermak of Chicago: A Study of Political Leadership* (Seattle: University of Washington Press, 1962); John V. Lindsay, *Journey into Politics: Some Informal Observations* (New York: Dodd, Mead, & Co., 1967) and *The City* (New York: W.W. Norton & Co., 1969); Henry W. Maier, *Challenge to the Cities: An Approach to a Theory of Urban Leadership* (New York: Random House, 1966); Martin Meyerson and Edward C. Banfield, *Politics, Planning, and the Public Interest: The Case of Public Housing in Chicago* (Glencoe, Ill.: The Free Press of Glencoe, 1955); Allan R. Talbot, *The Mayor's Game: Richard Lee of New Haven and the Politics of Change* (New York: Harper & Row, 1967); and Mike Royko, *Boss: Richard J. Daley of Chicago* (New York: E.P. Dutton & Co., 1971).

9. James V. Cunningham, *Urban Leadership in the Sixties* (Waltham, Mass.: Brandeis Univeristy, Lemberg Center for the Study of Violence, 1970).

10. David Rogers, *The Management of Big Cities: Interest Groups and Social Change Strategies* (Beverly Hills, Calif.: Sage Publications, 1971).

11. Alexander L. George, "Political Leadership and Social Change in American Cities," *Daedalus* 97 (Fall 1968), pp. 1194-1217.

12. J. David Greenstone and Paul E. Peterson, "Reformers, Machines, and the War on Poverty," in James Q. Wilson, ed. *City Politics and Public Policy* (New York: John Wiley & Sons, 1968), pp. 267-92.

13. See Robert H. Salisbury, "Urban Politics: The New Convergence of Power," *Journal of Politics* 26 (November 1964), pp. 775-97.

14. John P. Kotter and Paul R. Lawrence, "The Mayor: An Interim Research Report," a working paper distributed by the Division of Research, Graduate School of Business Administration, Harvard University, 1972.

15. The acceptance of a theoretical framework, or paradigm, for the analysis of a phenomena requires an implicit agreement among scholars about essential concepts, theoretical assumptions, and relationships. Vincent Ostrom observes: "Methods of work, conceptions of what is prob-

lematical, and criteria for what is to be included or excluded from the field of inquiry follow from a theoretical paradigm." See Vincent Ostrom, *The Intellectual Crisis in American Public Administration* (University, Alabama: University of Alabama Press, 1973), p. 13; and Thomas S. Kuhn, *The Structure of Scientific Revolutions* (Chicago: University of Chicago Press, 1962).

16. For a discussion of the characteristics and use of "theories of the middle range," see Robert K. Merton, *On Theoretical Sociology* (New York: The Free Press, 1967), especially pp. 39-53.

17. For a discussion of the use and limits of theories and models in comparative empirical inquiry, see Lawrence C. Mayer, *Comparative Political Inquiry* (Homewood, Ill.: Dorsey Press, 1972), especially pp. 48-66 and 102-42.

18. See Cecil A. Gibb, "Leadership—Psychological Aspects," *International Encyclopedia of the Social Sciences* 9 (New York: Macmillan Co., 1968), pp. 91-101.

19. See Daniel Katz and Robert L. Kahn, *The Social Psychology of Organizations* (New York, John Wiley & Sons, 1966) for a discussion of the operational difficulties of "leadership."

20. See the discussion of the relevance of power in the leadership process in Kenneth F. Janda, "Towards the Explication of the Concept of Leadership in Terms of the Concept of Power," *Human Relations* 13 (November 1960), pp. 345-63.

21. Glenn D. Paige identifies eleven distinct foci in leadership research: (1) studies of charisma; (2) didactic literature; (3) political biography and autobiography; (4) studies in leadership values and ideas; (5) studies in leadership styles; (6) institutional role studies; (7) political elite studies; (8) community power studies; (9) follower response studies; (10) area surveys; (11) leadership studies in other sociobehavioral sciences and applied fields. See his edited volume *Political Leadership: Readings for an Emerging Field* (New York: The Free Press, 1972), pp. 8-9.

22. Warren G. Bennis, "Leadership Theory and Administrative Behavior: The Problem of Authority," *Administrative Science Quarterly* 4 (December 1959), pp. 259-60.

23. See Donald D. Searing, "Models and Images of Man and Society in Leadership Theory," *Journal of Politics* 31 (February 1969), pp. 3-31.

24. Lewis J. Edinger, "Editor's Introduction," in Lewis J. Edinger, ed. *Political Leadership in Industrialized Societies* (New York: John Wiley & Sons, 1967), p. 5.

25. Ibid.

26. Ideally, the analysis of mayoral leadership effectiveness should take into consideration the outputs of the political system caused by the mayor; it should link outputs with behavior. There are two basic problems

associated with this kind of analysis: first, because there are many interven-
ing variables between a specific behavioral act and the system output (say
for educational expenditures), it is very difficult to identify and verify a
causal relationship between the input and output variables; second, the
comparability of outputs across systems also leaves much to be desired.
For example, a city's budget would seem to be a likely source for comparable data; however, expenditures are differently classified in different cities;
functions performed in one city by the general administration are performed in another by an independent board or commission; state and
federal grants-in-aid are a large portion of some cities' expenditures and a
small portion of others; and there are great differences in what services
money will buy in different jurisdictions.

27. See Lawrence B. Mohr, "The Concept of Organizational Goal,"
American Political Science Review 67 (June 1973), pp. 470-81.

28. The nondecision problem is a particularly explosive methodologi-
cal issue. For discussions of this problem, see the following articles and
accompanying journal correspondence: Peter Bachrach and Morton S.
Baratz, "The Two Faces of Power," *American Political Science Review* 56
(December 1962), pp. 947-52; and "Decisions and Non-decisions: An
Analytical Framework," *American Political Science Review* 57 (Sep-
tember 1963), pp. 632-42; Richard M. Merelman, "On the Neo-Elitist
Critique of Community Power," *American Political Science Review* 62
(June 1968), pp. 451-60; Raymond E. Wolfinger, "Nondecisions and the
Study of Local Politics," *American Political Science Review* 65 (December
1971), pp. 1063-80; and Frederick W. Frey, "Comment: On Issues and
Nonissues in the Study of Power," *American Political Science Review* 65
(December 1971), pp.1081-1101.

29. See Gary L. Wamsley and Mayer N. Zald, *The Political Economy
of Public Organizations: A Critique and Approach to the Study of Public
Administration* (Lexington, Mass.: Lexington Books, D.C. Heath, 1973)
for a discussion of the importance of politically relevant performance
criteria in public administration.

30. See Cunningham, *Urban Leadership in the Sixties,* p. 82.

31. See Jeffrey L. Pressman, "Preconditions of Mayoral Leadership,"
American Political Science Review 66 (June 1972), pp. 511-24.

32. See Dahl, *Who Governs?;* and Kotter and Lawrence, "The Mayor:
An Interim Research Report."

33. For a discussion of the use of "secondary criteria" in the broader
context of policy analysis, see Yehezkel Dror, *Public Policymaking
Re-examined* (San Francisco: Chandler Publishing Co., 1968), pp. 26-27.

34. "Necessary conditions" are properties that are required for an

event to occur, but an event will not take place unless "sufficient conditions," which are other requisites, are present. A condition can be both a necessary and a sufficient condition. For example, in Pressman's analysis of Oakland, "Preconditions of Mayoral Leadership," Mayor Reading lacked certain necessary conditions (resources) that made leadership difficult.

35. A discussion of these models is found in Kotter and Lawrence, "The Mayor: An Interim Research Report." The "business management" model is related to the reform movement and suggests that effective mayoral leadership will come from the recruitment of highly trained public servants who operate in a nonpartisan fashion. The "entrepreneur model" is best exemplified by Cunningham's model; the "political broker model," by Banfield's description of Mayor Daley; the "resources model," by Pressman's preconditions; and the "great man," "high energy" and "activist models" by newspaper accounts of New York City's Mayor John V. Lindsay. The "network model" is a creation of Kotter and Lawrence, but it is really an extension of earlier work by Talcott Parsons and Neil J. Smelser in *Economy and Society: A Study in the Integration of Economic and Sociological Theory* (Glencoe, Ill.: The Free Press of Glencoe, 1956) and interorganizational analysts.

36. See Cecil A. Gibb, "Leadership," in Gardner Lindzey, ed. *Handbook of Social Psychology* 2 (Reading, Mass.: Addison-Wesley Publishing Co., 1954), pp. 877-920.

37. This perspective is commonly used to define the concept of "political leadership." See Edinger, "Editor's Introduction," in *Political Leadership in Industrialized Societies*, pp. 1-25; and Katz and Kahn, *The Social Psychology of Organizations*, pp. 300-335.

38. Arthur L. Stinchcombe, *Constructing Social Theories* (New York: Harcourt, Brace & World, 1968), p. 189.

39. See George, "Political Leadership," p. 1206.

40. Perhaps the best descriptions of these types in the literature are Dahl's description of the "civic entrepreneur" in *Who Governs?*, Banfield's description of the "broker" in *Political Influence*, and Pressman's interpretation of nonleadership, or the "figurehead" form of mayoral leadership, in "Preconditions of Mayoral Leadership."

41. See Robert Tannenbaum, Irving R. Weschler, and Fred Massarik, *Leadership and Organization: A Behavioral Science Approach* (New York: McGraw-Hill Book Co., 1961).

42. This approach is taken in Marshall E. Dimock and Gladys O. Dimock, *Public Administration*, 4th ed. (New York: Holt, Rinehart & Winston, 1969), pp. 295-311; Andrew S. McFarland, *Power and Leader-*

ship in Pluralist Systems (Stanford, Calif.: Stanford University Press, 1969); and George, "Political Leadership and Social Change in American Cities."

43. See McFarland, *Power and Leadership in Pluralist Systems,* pp. 221-22.

44. See Stinchcombe, *Constructing Social Theories,* p. 189.

45. See Cunningham, *Urban Leadership in the Sixties,* p. 15.

46. Dahl, *Who Governs?,* p. 204.

47. Ibid., pp. 184-220.

48. Ibid., see also Pressman, "Preconditions of Mayoral Leadership"; Salisbury, "Urban Politics: The New Convergence of Power"; and George, "Political Leadership and Social Change in American Cities."

49. Salisbury, "Urban Politics: The New Convergence of Power," p. 787.

50. See George, "Political Leadership and Social Change in American Cities."

51. Contending with groups holding veto privileges in specific policy areas has been a continuing problem for mayors. This problem is perhaps best described in Sayre and Kaufman, *Governing New York City.*

52. Mayor Lee's marketing of his urban redevelopment program while mediating other community conflicts fits this model well. In addition to *Who Governs?,* see Talbot, *The Mayor's Game.*

53. See Sayre and Kaufman, *Governing New York City,* p. 716.

54. See Duane Lockard, *The Politics of State and Local Government,* 2nd ed. (New York: Macmillan Co., 1969), pp. 378-79; and Banfield, *Political Influence,* on the incentives to maintain a coalition rather than to innovate.

55. See George, "Political Leadership and Social Change in American Cities," p. 1206.

56. See Banfield, *Political Influence,* pp. 270-71. According to Banfield, Mayor Daley's reluctance to exert authority in some conflictual situations reflected the widely shared view that in Chicago, "a policy ought to be framed by the interests affected, not by the political head or his agents."

57. See David Braybrooke, "The Mystery of Executive Success Reexamined," *Administrative Science Quarterly* 8 (March 1964), pp. 533-60.

58. For a discussion of the confusion in political psychology that is relevant to leadership, see Fred I. Greenstein, "The Impact of Personality on Politics: An Attempt to Clear Away Underbrush," *American Political Science Review* 61 (September 1967), pp. 629-41.

59. James D. Barber, "Editor's Introduction," in James D. Barber, ed.

Leadership in American Government (Boston: Little, Brown, & Co., 1964), p. 6.

60. James D. Barber, "Classifying and Predicting Presidential Styles: Two 'Weak' Presidents," *Journal of Social Issues* 24 (July 1968), p. 52.

61. See Cunningham, *Urban Leadership in the Sixties,* p. 13.

62. Ibid., p. 82.

63. Ibid., p. 15.

64. Cunningham's analysis suffers from some serious limitations. His analysis is essentially individualistic and underemphasizes the importance of resources, goals, and context as factors conditioning leadership. It also suffers from a liberal bias that equates leadership with integration and change. In the case of Cleveland's Mayor Locher, it appears that minimum change was a sought-after goal. His ability to avoid decision making and change in Cleveland indicates a substantial degree of influence in pursuit of a goal. Finally, by minimizing differences between cities, Cunningham was able to control for context, but lost the opportunity to examine relationships between style and circumstance.

65. Jeffrey L. Pressman, "Preconditions of Mayoral Leadership," paper delivered at the Sixty-Sixth Annual Meeting of The American Political Science Association, Los Angeles, September 8-12, 1970, pp. 2-3.

66. For a discussion of collective goods and leadership, see Norman Frohlich, Joe A. Oppenheimer, and Oran R. Young, *Political Leadership and Collective Goods* (Princeton, N.J.: Princeton University Press, 1971).

67. Ibid., p. 3; see also Mancur Olson, Jr., *The Logic of Collective Action: Public Goods and the Theory of Groups* (Cambridge, Mass.: Harvard University Press, 1965) for a discussion of the role of side payments in the provision of public goods.

68. See Kotter and Lawrence, "The Mayor," p. 31.

69. The importance of financial slack in promoting a climate conducive to innovations has been examined by Lawrence B. Mohr in "Determinants of Innovation in Organization," *American Political Science Review* 62 (March 1969), pp. 111-26.

70. See Pressman, "Preconditions of Mayoral Leadership."

71. See Kotter and Lawrence, "The Mayor," pp. 27-33. Similar propositions also have been proposed by exchange and compliance theorists, like Amitai Etzioni, *A Comparative Analysis of Complex Organizations: On Power, Involvement and Their Correlates* (New York: The Free Press, 1961); Peter Blau, *Exchange and Power in Social Life* (New York: John Wiley & Sons, 1964); and George C. Homans, *Social Behavior: Its Elementary Forms* (New York: Harcourt, Brace & World, 1961).

72. The author was inspired to use "polarity," "harmony," "integra-

tion," and "constraint in conflicts" as variables after reading Eulau and Prewitt, *Labyrinths of Democracy,* especially chapter 9.

73. See Kotter and Lawrence, "The Mayor," pp. 23-27.

74. Rogers, *The Management of Big Cities,* p. 9.

75. McFarland, *Power and Leadership in Pluralist Systems,* pp. 225-26.

76. See, for example, William C. Mitchell, "Occupational Role Strains: The American Elective Public Official," *Administrative Science Quarterly* 3 (September 1958), pp. 210-28.

77. See Jackson Toby, "Some Variables in Role Conflict Analysis," *Social Forces* 30 (March 1952), pp. 323-27; and Michael Lipsky, *Protest in City Politics: Rent Strikes, Housing and the Power of the Poor* (Chicago: Rand McNally & Co., 1970), pp. 175-81.

78. See McFarland, *Power and Leadership in Pluralist Systems,* pp. 210-16.

79. Ibid., p. 217.

80. Ibid., p. 218.

81. Ibid., p. 219.

82. See George, "Political Leadership and Social Change in American Cities," p. 1212.

83. For a discussion of the use of rancorous and obstructionist tactics in political conflicts, see Stuart M. Schmidt and Thomas A. Kochan, "Conflict: Toward Conceptual Clarity," *Administrative Science Quarterly* 17 (September 1972), pp. 359-70; and William A. Gamson, "Rancorous Conflict in Community Politics," *American Sociological Review* 31 (January 1966), pp. 71-81.

84. See William A. Gamson, "Stable Unrepresentation in American Society," *American Behavioral Scientist* 12 (November-December 1968), pp. 15-21; and Robert A. Dahl, *Pluralist Democracy in the United States: Conflict and Consensus* (Chicago: Rand McNally & Co., 1967).

85. For some informed discussions of the fiscal "crunch" in American cities, see John P. Crecine, ed. *Financing the Metropolis: Public Policy in Urban Economies* (Beverly Hills, Calif.: Sage Publications, 1970).

86. For a discussion of the decline of collective goods under conditions of societal conflict, see Alvin Rabushka and Kenneth A. Shepsle, "Political Entrepreneurship and Patterns of Democratic Instability in Plural Societies," *Race* 12 (April 1971), pp. 461-76.

87. Ibid., also Alvin Rabushka and Kenneth A Shepsle, *Politics in Plural Societies: A Theory of Democratic Instability* (Columbus, Ohio: Chas. E. Merrill Publishing Co., 1972).

88. See Joseph S. Himes, "The Functions of Racial Conflict," *Social Forces* 45 (September 1966), pp. 1-10.

89. For a discussion of the threat of co-optation to the "black power movement," see Stokely Carmichael and Charles V. Hamilton, *Black Power: The Politics of Liberation in America* (New York: Random House, 1967).

90. For example, criticisms by black spokesmen of public policies such as the Vietnam War, the space program, and environmental protection programs are often made in terms of their opportunity costs to the economic development of the black community.

91. See Harold Baron, "Black Powerlessness in Chicago," *Trans-action* 6 (November 1968), pp. 27-33; James Q. Wilson, "Two Negro Politicians: An Interpretation," *Midwest Journal of Political Science* 4 (November 1960), pp. 346-69; and *Negro Politics: The Search for Leadership* (New York: The Free Press, 1960). Also Matthew A. Crenson, *The Un-Politics of Air Pollution: A Study of Non-Decision Making in the Cities* (Baltimore: Johns Hopkins Press, 1971), especially p. 56 for a discussion of the passivity of black councilmen in Gary during the 1950s.

92. See Rabushka and Shepsle, *Politics in Plural Societies;* also Murray Edelman, "Escalation and Ritualization of Political Conflict," *American Behavioral Scientist* 13 (November-December 1969), pp. 231-46.

93. See Cunningham, *Urban Leadership in the Sixties,* p. 13.

3 Racial Conflict as a Constraint and an Opportunity for Mayoral Leadership

Models of executive effectiveness based exclusively on experience in pluralist contexts are inappropriate when applied to other types of situational contexts. Since racial polarization produces a nonpluralistic context, efforts by mayors to build executive-centered coalitions or adopt collective-goods postures are likely to fail. The biases of pluralist analysis and the failure of the urban literature to provide models of mayoral leadership applicable to different situational contexts, particularly those contexts involving racial polarization, suggest the need for an alternative approach. The rudiments of such an alternative approach may be found in the literature on community conflict and cultural pluralism.

A recurring controversy is found throughout the literature on the four central concepts considered in this book: leadership, race relations, pluralism, and public policy. The controversy concerns the use and interpretation of these concepts and has often involved two alternative and usually mutually exclusive images of man and society: order and conflict.[1] In both images or frameworks, a plurality of groups provides the basis for the analysis of communities. However, in order frameworks the autonomy of groups and institutions promotes a dispersion of power and a competition between groups that results in a relatively peaceful dynamic equilibrium.[2] Pluralist leadership models are very congruent with order frameworks. Thus, Pressman, after constructing a pluralist "ideal" model of mayoral leadership, writes that the "ideal mayor might strive to maintain within the political system a process of constructive dialogue between diverse groups which would contribute to harmony in the city."[3]

In order frameworks, political integration (and ultimately the formation of executive-centered coalitions) depends upon functional interdependence between groups, common values, and cross-cutting allegiances.[4] In conflict frameworks, by contrast, "independence of the cultural sections implies dissolution of the society; intersectional conflict threatens the very existence of the society."[5] In conflict models, "the binding mechanism is governmental regulation and ultimately force."[6] In short, order frameworks view social diversity as functional to democratic competition, political integration, and social stability. Conflict frameworks view diversity as dysfunctional to democracy because it may lead to the subordination of "minority" groups, the generation of intergroup conflict, and eventually may create conditions that lead to societal instability.

Order images, frameworks, and models have dominated the empirical theory of American social science. As has been argued, the literature of mayoral leadership, community decision making, and public policy has reflected the biases of an order framework, pluralist analysis. Even the field of race relations reflects an order bias. As Van den Berghe argues, this field "has been dominated by a functionalist view of society and a definition of the race problem as one of integration and assimilation of minorities into a mainstream of a consensus-based society."[7] When viewed from an order perspective, American blacks are seen as one of many ethnic groups in a universe of interest groups with shared memberships and similar sociopolitical outlooks, competing for similar political stakes within established rules of the game.

The limitations of using pluralist or order models to analyze American race relations are particularly striking in the context of local politics. Recent studies of the attitudes and experiences of black and white urban residents reveal major differences in their outlooks, perceptions, and expectations toward local political issues, institutions, and officeholders.[8] These studies disclose that many blacks prefer new policies of a nonroutine nature, feel oppressed, and believe that rancorous forms of conflict are appropriate political strategies.[9] In communities with large black populations holding these attitudes, dissensus dominates local politics. The cleavages between blacks and whites in local politics render order models inappropriate as explanatory tools to understand urban racial politics. A conflict framework provides a more useful conceptualization.

Conflict frameworks assume sociopolitical disagreement and dissensus. In conflict frameworks, two or more groups are separated from one another by territory, class, caste, social position, race, or religion.[10] The cause of the separation or segregation is usually rooted in the society's history. The factions share a common government.[11] In conflict frameworks groups are crystallized and conscious of their separateness and distinctiveness.[12] Cleavages are cumulative and parallel, and mutually exclusive institutions and memberships exist within the segments or groups of the society.[13] A dominant-subordinate relationship exists or has existed between the groups or segments. From a conflict perspective, American blacks are viewed not as one of many ethnic or interest groups, but are seen instead as a historically unique segment that is emerging from a position as a subordinated racial group with a relatively substantial degree of political power, distinctly different political goals, and an infrastructure of relatively viable and separate political institutions.[14] This interpretation of racial politics has important significance for understanding urban politics and the future prospects of the American mayoralty.

Since the early 1960s black political mobilization has created new demands on urban governments and has found new forms of political expression. Increased black political activity and the adoption of unconventional political tactics helped to increase black political power and produced advances in public services and economic opportunity. However, these tactics and successes alerted urban white communities and produced a countermobilization that led to increased recalcitrance on the part of many city bureaucracies and administrators.[15] Victories by "law and order" mayoral candidates, who symbolized white resistance and hostility to black advances, serve as an indicator of the power of countermobilization in white-dominated, racially polarized communities.[16]

Racial polarization in many American cities also helps to explain the demise of white liberal mayors and political immobilism. While white liberal mayors have been caught between black impatience and white resistance, black mayors are only partially freed from the conflict of racial expectations that makes the mayoralty in racially polarized communities so unstable. The symbolic significance of a black mayor and the new programs he is able to produce appear to satisfy most of his black constituents.[17] But the hostility of the white community often constrains the black mayor who attempts to exert influential communitywide leadership through conventional pluralist leadership strategies. In a racially polarized community, a black mayor's leadership problems are similar to the problems encountered by a white liberal mayor.

In short, the politics of a number of American cities have become polarized along racial lines, superimposing the issue of race upon almost every significant political issue.[18]

In these communities, politics involves two factions formed in stable coalitions.[19] Political strategy frequently involves rancorous and obstructionist tactics.[20] By contrast, in pluralist systems, politics is characterized by multilateral competition, shifting coalitions, and is relatively devoid of "such tactics as threats of punishment, personal vilification, and deliberate conscious deceptions."[21] Given the salience of community conflict patterns for mayoral leadership, and the domination of the literature by the pluralist model, we must consider the problem of identifying the forms of mayoral leadership that emerge in racially polarized communities. Closely linked to this question is the problem of conceptualizing a form of mayoral leadership that is effective in these communities.

Conflict Patterns in Pluralized and Polarized Systems

In every community there is some competition and conflict associated with the activities and plans of local government. The pattern of conflict offers constraints, problems, and opportunities for mayoral leadership. These conflict patterns are shaped by the social composition of the community, its

Table 3-1
The Properties of Pluralized and Polarized Systems

	Pluralized Systems	Polarized Systems
Social Composition:	heterogeneous	bifurcated
Polarity:	multipolar	bipolar
Conflict Relationships:	multilateral	bilateral
Group Memberships:	Overlapping and cross-cutting	cumulative and superimposed
Political Culture:	diverse, but basically shared	divergent
Conflict Behavior:	conventional, within the "rules of the games"	rancorous
Mediating and Integrating Influences:	political party or economic elite	none
Patterns of Transactions between Factions:	positive sum, joint payoffs	zero sum

polarity, conflict relationships, group memberships, political culture, conflict behavior, patterns of transactions between factions, and the existence and power of mediating and integrating influences.[22] Using these eight dimensions, it is possible to differentiate analytically between the two basic contexts of urban politics: pluralized and polarized systems.

In heterogeneous communities, politics tend toward pluralism in its many variations, because as the complexity of a community's socioeconomic and ethnic structure increases from horizontal and vertical differentiation, the number of separate interests competing in the political arena also increases.[23] In communities of this type, there are numerous ethnic and economic minority groups, cleavages are cross-cutting, and interest groups tend to specialize in specific issue areas. Politics is performed primarily by the representatives of organized interest groups to serve the maintenance needs of these organizations.[24] The elites carrying out the political struggle tend to support the prevailing norms of political competition, and conflict is further mediated by either a strong political party or a group of economic elites, who promote mutually beneficial compromises.

In contrast, a polarized community is split by a deep cleavage along a single dimension; a cleavage between two opposing groups in a community is superimposed on all conflicts in the community. Communities may be divided by race, religion, class, or ideology. When conflicts involve the same antagonists on a broad number of issues and leaders are identical and identifiable on many issues, politics tend to be rancorous and to have zero-sum outcomes.

In this circumstance there is no conflict regulation mechanism because mediating groups like political machines do not exist to span the conflict. One group perceives the other as a threat to its property, status, and power; and the other perceives its adversaries as blocking its economic and social mobility.[25] In effect, in this kind of situation, to know either a man's race, or his religion, or his job is to know his political party, his place of residence, his clubs, church, education, even his favorite foods and restaurants. Generally, this kind of situation is characterized by a breakdown of traditional patterns of class and caste.

These two types of communities are dichotomized "ideal types" that will not be found in pristine form in reality. However, real communities will tend to fulfill the conditions of one type rather than the other. So, while it is impossible to find any communities that exactly fit either pattern, it is possible to specify that a community more closely resembles one of the two.[26]

Both of these situations provide aspiring politicians with different opportunity structures and make different kinds of demands on candidates and incumbents for performance and policy output. These different opportunity patterns will be attractive to different types of people, and the exploitation of their opportunities will result in different recruitment and policy patterns.

Conflict Patterns as Opportunity Structures

A useful approach to studying the interaction between contextual properties and the mayoral role is to view the impact of a city's political and social structure on patterns of mayoral recruitment and succession. The structural approach concentrates on "the relationships in a social situation which limit the choice process to a particular range of alternatives."[27] Using a structural perspective expands the definition of a situation from a short-run examination of the dynamics of a particular issue to a broader view of the community's social and organizational structure. As issues, cleavages, ethnic balances, and power relationships change, the opportunities presented to potential mayors also change. Using this approach, it is possible to better understand how the style of a mayor is responsive or congruent to the demands of a particular type of context. This is not to say that the situation entirely determines the man who is recruited into the mayoralty or his behavior once in office; rather, the probabilities for certain types of men and styles to emerge are greater under certain types of circumstances than others.[28]

Analyzing recruitment and performance from an opportunity perspective highlights the importance of the role expectations of incumbents and constituents. An office's opportunity structure includes not only the formal rules of selection, but also the willingness of certain types of people to seek the office and the willingness of voters to accept the candidacy of the office seeker.[29] Therefore, the opportunity structure for recruitment into a specific office includes the formal rules of selection, the party systems that serve a gatekeeping function to narrow the field of viable candidates, and the performance, background, and policy preferences of voters.

The opportunity structure approach is particularly relevant to understanding mayoral recruitment and performance because of the changing demographic and organizational characteristics of many American cities. The growth of the central city's black population and its increasing political power has created new blends of political opportunities for ambitious urban politicians, both black and white. From the perspective of the black politician, the percentage of black voters in a commumity is an indicator of his opportunity for office. Likewise, the white politician will assess his chances for office on the size and militancy of the white population and on the congruence of the appeals needed to win election with his long-term ambitions and personal beliefs. This is not to say that a politician cannot influence the structure of a situation to increase his political opportunities; rather, this approach assumes that a politician calculating his political future will run for offices he can win and, when elected, can manage (unless he has been promised another office or appointment if he runs a strong race); and under different kinds of circumstances, different kinds of people will be induced to seek an office.

In American urban politics there are currently two facts of life: first, blacks and whites are "separate and unequal;"[30] second, both groups know it. The consciousness of inequality presents a deep cleavage in urban communities that aspiring politicians have exploited in lieu of building broad support across races to assemble winning coalitions. Black politicians have exploited black pride and identity and hatred toward whites to mobilize large blocs of black votes, while white voters have been aroused by white candidates to turn back the threat of black power and control. Under polarized conditions, political conflict will be intense and the means of conflict will extend beyond the normal "rules of the game."[31]

Polarity requires organization. Factions must be mobilized and organized in order to be potent political forces.[32] Once mobilized into factions, the conflict potential in a community rises.[33] As the level of conflict in a community rises, the conflict surrounding the mayoral role also rises, because there is increased likelihood of disagreement between the conflicting groups about the proper role, legitimacy, and behavior of the mayor. Even though all the necessary conditions are present for rancorous conflict, it takes an act by an individual to provide sufficient conditions for a conflict.[34] Whether the precipitating act is performed by the mayor or another community leader, the issue will often be defined by the activity and partisanship of the mayor as the central actor in the local political system.[35] In many controversial local issues like school desegregation, the location of public housing, fluoridation, and the administration of federal programs, the mayor has become the focal figure for much of the controversy.

Conflict over the behavior of a mayor will frequently develop when a mayor does not conform to rigidly held role expectations because he holds a differing set of allegiances to groups other than traditional community influentials, because a new group has arisen making new performance demands, or because he fails to perform duties that have become associated with the role over time.[36] Conflict levels rise when role expectations are solidified and disappointed. Since role expectations are more intense and therefore more solidified in a polarized community, conflict surrounding the mayoral role is also likely to be more intense.

An aspiring mayor will make a run/no run decision based on two factors: his chances of winning an election and his satisfaction with the demands and rewards of the office. Even under the most favorable conditions, knowing that the mayoral role is complex and involves the assumption of a variety of thankless tasks will often discourage people from seeking the mayoralty. When these roles are complicated by the strains and pressures of intense racial conflict, many highly qualified potential candidates decide the mayorship is more a bother than a political opportunity.

Mayoral Leadership as Bystandership, Partisanship, and Hegemonyship

Three types of leadership models emerged from the discussion of mayoral leadership in pluralistic communities: the civic entrepreneur, the broker, and the figurehead. By using the same four criteria to classify leadership in polarized communities that were developed to evaluate mayoral performance in pluralistic communities—mobilization, innovation, centralization, and integration—three new types of mayoral leadership can be identified: the *bystander,* the *partisan,* and the *hegemonic* style.

The bystander model of mayoral leadership is not uncommon in American cities polarized along racial lines. Unable to find an overarching program or to integrate the two racial groups into a centralizing coalition, a number of mayors have calculated that overt partisanship is distasteful, unfeasible, or damaging to their political futures. Buffered by the intense hostility of the struggle between racial groups, some mayors have chosen to evade proposals initiated by either side, discard any innovative ideas of their own, and simply maintain present levels of traditional services. A mayor who chooses a bystander strategy does little more than view the conflict going on about him.

A number of other mayors have chosen to become partisans in urban racial conflict, openly favoring one side over the other. Many mayors are elected and reelected primarily because of their racial positions, usually articulated in a vague rhetoric that nevertheless conveys precise meaning to their constituencies. For example, a number of white mayors have been elected on "law and order" platforms that were easily translated to mean opposition to school integration, scattered-site public housing, improved welfare benefits, ghetto development, and equal employment opportunity for blacks. In cities where mayors have behaved as partisans, conflict has often been exacerbated and politics has become rancorous. Under conditions of racial polarization, a mayor choosing a partisan orientation focuses politics on the mayoralty. Innovations are constrained within the limits imposed by the opposition faction's veto powers. Where whites have been dominant, mayoral policy has often been oriented towards reaffirming the status quo or returning to the state of affairs that existed before blacks won some policy concessions.[37] Where blacks have been dominant, mayoral policy has tended to be biased in favor of blacks but has often been constrained by media and public opinion, provisions in state and federal grant agreements, and a multiplicity of veto points at higher levels of government where whites have superior access and sympathetic allies.[38]

In short, a mayor adopting the partisan model of mayoral leadership centralizes politics, presses for marginal innovations in policy (or redirects trends in policy change to reestablish an earlier state of affairs), and builds a coalition composed almost exclusively of members of his own racial group. The only members of his coalition and administration of the other racial group are "token" and minority members who are included for their symbolic, financial, or technical value or whose political power cannot be ignored.[39] Since communitywide mobilization and political integration are not goals of the partisan mayor, he strives to solidify his personal political position and to mobilize his racial group, hoping to attain a long-term political hegemony in the community.

A polar alternative to the pluralist's civic entrepreneur model of highly effective mayoral leadership is the hegemonic style of leadership in polarized communities. In the history of the United States, strong mayoral leadership has occasionally been achieved in high cleavage communities. For example, in many southern cities white mayors leading or participating in all-white coalitions have dominated blacks, excluding them from even the benefits of traditional services.[40] In the North, during periods of ethnic succession and ascendancy, some mayors assembled dominant coalitions and dispensed political rewards exclusively to members of their faction. A similar scenario can be drawn for a number of American cities as blacks ascend to overwhelming numerical and political dominance. In this context, a black mayor may develop an effective black political machine. If blacks comprise a large enough political force, such a coalition may exclude whites from political benefits and still win elections. This form of partisan posture will accelerate the exodus of whites from the city and spur hostile rear-guard obstructionist tactics from white politicians. Under conditions of intense racially oriented political conflict, the dominant position of the mayor and his all-black coalition is strengthened, as racial appeals can be used to mobilize black voters. The mayor will be in the position of leading a tightly integrated organization and will be able, within the constraints of his resources, legality, jurisdiction, and the goodwill of the state and federal government, to activate almost any innovative program he chooses irrespective of the media or white opinion. The programs themselves will not be of a collective-goods nature but, instead, will be aimed at providing services, jobs, and political rewards exclusively to the mayor's black constituents. When this form of mayoral leadership occurs, a high degree of mayoral influence will exist, the resources of the community will be mobilized, politics will be centralized in the mayoralty, but the hegemonic coalition that governs the city will integrate only blacks, excluding whites.

In summary, under conditions of community polarization, a high degree of mayoral influence is possible when a mayor adopts a partisan posture *and* leads a dominant faction that controls the community's governmental machinery. Furthermore, if polarization makes pluralist politics and the creation of an executive-centered coalition impossible, another path to influential mayoral leadership that minimizes the constraints of racial polarization may be through the creation of a hegemonic coalition that attains exclusive control of the policy-making process.

The Special Case of Consociation

While polarization tends to produce either immobilist or hegemonic regimes, these two outcomes are not inexorable. Another outcome is possible: a consociation, a fragmented but stable democracy that includes subcultures divided by reinforcing cleavages. In these societies, Lijphart observes, political elites "make deliberate efforts to counteract the immobilizing and unstabilizing effects of cultural fragmentation."[41] A consociational democracy is "government by elite cartel designed to turn a democracy with a fragmented political culture into a stable democracy."[42]

In analyzing regimes that fit the consociational pattern (Switzerland,

Austria, Lebanon, and the Low Countries), Lijphart specifies four preconditions for successful consociational democracy:

(1) That the elites have the ability to accommodate the divergent interests and
demands of the subcultures. (2) This requires that they have the ability to transcend
cleavages and to join in a common effort with the elites of rival subcultures. (3) This
in turn depends on their commitment to the maintenance of the system and to the
improvement of its cohesion and stability. (4) Finally, all of the above requirements
are based on the assumption that the elites understand the perils of political
fragmentation.[43]

These preconditions involve three kinds of interrelationships: inter-
subcultural relations at the elite level, inter-subcultural relations at the
mass level, and elite-mass relations within each of the subcultures. In other
words, when elites cooperate with one another across cleavages and effectively represent quiescent masses, a consociational arrangement may result.

Consociational regimes take many different forms. They may involve
coalition cabinets, multimember executives, coalition committees, rota-
tion of ethnic group representatives in top executive offices, informal
councils, agreements not to contest certain elections, and other extraordinary procedures that provide mechanisms for overarching cooperation at
the elite level. "The essential characteristic of consociational democracy is
not so much any particular institutional arrangement as the deliberate joint
effort by the elites to stabilize the system."[44]

In consociational regimes interelite cooperation is bolstered by previous successful cooperative experiences, external threats, a multiple balance of power among subcultures rather than a dual balance or hegemony,
little hope by one faction that it will eventually become dominant, and a
relatively low total load on the decision-making apparatus. Further, clear
boundaries among subcultures, with no close contact or competition for
jobs, status or space, also promotes consociation. "Hence, it may be desirable
to keep transactions among antagonistic subcultures in a divided
society—or similarly, among different nationalities in a multinational
state—to a minimum."[45]

Consociation is fostered by a high degree of internal political cohesion
within the subcultures, because elites must be able to count on the loyalty
of members of their group's rank and file to build binding bargains and
compromises. For elites to gain the allegiance and support of members of
their subculture, there must be a widespread approval of the principal of
government by elite cartel and faith in the responsiveness of each
subgroup's elite to its rank and file.

While consociations promise a way out of the bind of immobilism and
sporadic intergroup conflict, they nevertheless still promote a certain degree of immobilism by allowing concurrent majorities to veto redistributive

proposals and by narrowing policy agendas to collective-goods programs and distributive bargaining. Executive leadership is also limited in consociational arrangements. We know little of the functioning of prime ministers and presidents in consociational regimes, but the concept itself, rule by elite cartel, implies executives functioning largely as figureheads symbolically representing their subcultural group. In this kind of a system, elites negotiate policy, and the executive's role is bounded by statute, custom, and his informal power within his subcultural group.

The consociation appears to be an attractive alternative to the immobilism plaguing American cities. However, the political dynamics of many cities fail to provide the preconditions that promote successful consociational democracy. There are a number of reasons for the absence of elite cooperation in American cities. First, the powers of city governments are limited and a breakdown in decision-making processes will not greatly imperil urban life, although crises like strikes by municipal employees and outbreaks of rioting may occasionally inconvenience the majority of local citizens. Second, given the limited consequences of political fragmentation, ambitious politicians may see more opportunity than danger in exacerbating conflict and fragmentation than in seeking compromise. Third, cooperation often presents the danger of being charged with "selling out" to the enemy and may endanger the position of subcultural elites within their group. Fourth, divergent personal goals and subgroup ambitions may negate dialogue between elites of rival subcultures. Fifth, intragroup competition for leadership positions and intrafactional strife may demand that elites devote all their energies to maintaining their power and leave little time for intergroup cooperation. Sixth, rapid turnover of elites may interrupt a stream of compromises, rendering some agreements void and others more problematic. Seventh, demographic changes may make it apparent that one group will become dominant in the future. Eighth, external threats may not be present. Ninth, the demands on government may be so heavy that the time needed for bargaining may simply not be available. Finally, and most importantly, the subcultures may be in close contact and in competition for housing, jobs, and status, promoting antagonistic transactions between members of the subcultural groups.

Given these limitations, observers of American urban politics should not be overly optimistic about the chances of consociational regimes developing in our cities in the near future. In spite of the existence of biracial cooperative politics in some cities like Atlanta, which, at times has resembled a consociational form, racial antipathy in most municipalities tends to create too many centrifugal forces for consociations to persist.

In communities governed by elite cartels, mayoral leadership is limited by the necessity to engage in continuous rounds of ad hoc bargaining. Given the multiplicity of veto points and the informal nature of political decision making, policy initiatives are limited to relatively marginal changes in local policy and ecology. Under conditions of consociation, immobilism is avoided, but mayoral leadership tends to involve only limited amounts of centralization, integration, mobilization, and innovation.

Notes

1. See Donald D. Searing, "Models and Images of Man and Society in Leadership Theory," *Journal of Politics* 31 (February 1969), pp. 3-31; Dennis H. Wrong, "The Oversocialized Conception of Man in Modern Sociology." *American Sociological Review* 26 (April 1961), pp. 183-93; John Horton, "Order and Conflict Theories of Social Problems as Competing Ideologies," *American Journal of Sociology* 71 (May 1966), pp. 701-13; and Pierre L. Van den Berghe, "Dialectic and Functionalism: Toward a Theoretical Synthesis," *American Sociological Review* 28 (October 1963), pp. 695-705.

2. See Leo Kuper and M.G. Smith, eds. *Pluralism in Africa* (Berkeley: University of California Press, 1969); Pierre L. Van den Berghe, *Race and Racism: A Comparative Perspective* (New York: John Wiley & Sons, 1967); and *Race* 12 (April 1971).

3. Jeffrey L. Pressman, "Preconditions of Mayoral Leadership," *American Political Science Review* 66 (June 1972), p. 512.

4. See Van den Berghe, "Dialectic and Functionalism: Toward a Theoretical Synthesis" in *Race and Racism*.

5. Leo Kuper, "Plural Societies: Perspectives and Problems," in *Pluralism in Africa*, p. 17.

6. Ibid.

7. Van den Berghe, *Race and Racism*, p. 7.

8. See Gary T. Marx, *Protest and Prejudice: A Study of Belief in the Black Community* (New York: Harper & Row, 1967); Angus Campbell and Howard Schuman, "Racial Attitudes in Fifteen American Cities" in *Supplemental Studies for the National Advisory Commission on Civil Disorders* (Washington, D.C.: Government Printing Office, 1968); and Joel D. Aberbach and Jack L. Walker, "Attitudes of Blacks and Whites Toward City Services: Implications for Public Policy," in John P. Crecine, ed. *Financing the Metropolis: Public Policy in Urban Economics* (Beverly Hills, Calif.: Sage Publications, 1970), pp. 519-38; and *Race In the City* (Boston: Little, Brown & Co., 1973); Charles S. Bullock, III and Harrell R. Rodgers, Jr., eds. *Black Political Attitudes: Implications for Political Support* (Chicago: Markham Publishing Co., 1972).

9. See T.M. Tomlinson, "The Development of a Riot Ideology among Urban Negroes," *American Behavioral Scientist* 11 (March-April 1968),

pp. 27-3l; and Robert M. Fogelson and Robert B. Hill, "Who Riots? A Study of Participation in the 1967 Riots" in *Supplemental Studies*, pp. 217-43.

10. See Alvin Rabushka and Kenneth A. Shepsle, *Politics in Plural Societies: A Theory of Democratic Instability* (Columbus, Ohio: Chas. E. Merrill Publishing Co., 1972).

11. See Richard Rose, *Governing Without Consensus: An Irish Perspective* (Boston: Beacon Press, 1971).

12. See Douglas W. Rae amd Michael Taylor, *The Analysis of Political Cleavages* (New Haven: Yale University Press, 1970), p. 24.

13. See Kuper and Smith, *Pluralism in Africa*.

14. See Van den Berghe, *Race and Racism*, pp. 77-95, and "Pluralism and the Polity: A Theoretical Exploration," in *Pluralism in Africa*, pp. 67-81.

15. See Jewell Bellush and Stephen M. David, eds. *Race and Politics in New York City* (New York: Praeger Publishers, 1971); and Michael Lipsky, *Protest in City Politics: Rent Strikes, Housing and the Power of the Poor* (Chicago: Rand McNally & Co., 1970).

16. Examples are the elections of Frank Rizzo in Philadelphia and Ralph Perk in Cleveland. See James Q. Wilson and Harold R. Wilde, "The Urban Mood," *Commentary* 48 (October 1969), pp. 52-61; and Fred Powledge, "Flight from City Hall," *Harper's Magazine* 239 (November 1969), pp. 69-86.

17. See James Q. Wilson, "The Mayors vs. The Cities," *Public Interest* 16 (Summer 1969), p. 35.

18. The concept of "superimposition" comes from Ralf Dahrendorf, *Class and Class Conflict in Industrial Society* (Stanford, Calif.: Stanford University Press, 1959).

19. See Rabushka and Shepsle, *Politics in Plural Societies*.

20. See William A. Gamson, "Rancorous Conflict in Community Politics," *American Sociological Review* 31 (February 1966), p. 71; and Stuart M. Schmidt and Thomas A. Kochan, "Conflict: Toward Conceptual Clarity," *Administrative Science Quarterly* 17 (September 1972), pp. 359-70.

21. Gamson, "Rancorous Conflict in Community Politics," p.71.

22. See Robert A. Dahl, *Democracy in the United States: Promise and Performance*, 2nd ed. (Chicago: Rand McNally & Co., 1972), pp. 310-12 for a reasonably similar analytical dichotomization of the properties of communities that promote or constrain conflict.

23. See John Walton, "Differential Patterns of Community Power Structure: An Explanation Based on Interdependence," in Terry N. Clark, ed. *Community Structure and Decision-Making: Comparative Analyses* (San Francisco: Chandler Publishing Co., 1968), pp. 441-59.

24. See Edward C. Banfield, *Political Influence* (New York: The Free Press, 1961), pp. 263-85.

25. See Dahrendorf, *Class and Class Conflict*, pp. 206-40.

26. For an insightful discussion of the use of ideal types for comparative and theoretical purposes, see Abraham Kaplan, *The Conduct of Inquiry: Methodology for Behavioral Science* (San Francisco: Chandler Publishing Co., 1964), pp. 82-83.

27. Andrew S. McFarland, *Power and Leadership in Pluralist Systems* (Stanford, Calif.: Stanford University Press, 1969), p. 134.

28. See Joseph A. Schlesinger, *Ambition and Politics: Political Careers in the United States* (Chicago: Rand McNally & Co., 1966); Kenneth Prewitt, "Political Ambitions, Volunteerism and Electoral Accountability," *American Political Science Review* 64 (March 1970), pp. 5-17; and Donald S. Bradley and Mayer N. Zald, "From Commercial Elite to Political Administrator: The Recruitment of the Mayors of Chicago," *American Journal of Sociology* (September 1965), pp. 153-67.

29. See Lester G. Seligman, "Political Parties and the Recruitment of Political Leadership," Lewis J. Edinger, ed. *Political Leadership in Industrialized Societies* (New York: John Wiley & Sons, 1967), pp. 294-315.

30. National Advisory Commission on Civil Disorders, *Report* (Washington, D.C.: Government Printing Office, 1967), p. 1.

31. See Gamson, "Rancorous Conflict in Community Politics."

32. See David B. Truman, *The Governmental Process: Political Interests and Public Opinion* (New York: Alfred A. Knopf, 1951); and Mancur Olson, Jr., *The Logic of Collective Action: Public Goods and the Theory of Groups* (Cambridge, Mass.: Harvard University Press, 1965).

33. There are two views on this proposition. One holds that organized factions will be more likely to engage in conflict behavior to promote their interests, thus causing instability. The other view argues that the elites of organized factions will avoid conflict, maintain their power, and promote societal stability. For examples of these two views, see William A. Gamson, *Power and Discontent* (Homewood, Ill.: Dorsey Press, 1968); and Murray Edelman, *Politics as Symbolic Action: Mass Arousal and Quiescence* (Chicago: Markham Publishing Co., 1971).

34. See Norton E. Long, "The Political Act as an Act of Will," *American Journal of Sociology* 69 (July 1963), pp. 1-6.

35. Many studies of community politics discuss the mayor as the symbolic head and focal point of city politics. Among the best discussions of this phenomena in the literature are: Robert L. Crain, Elihu Katz, and Donald B. Rosenthal, *The Politics of Community Conflict: The Fluoridation Decision* (Indianapolis: Bobbs-Merrill Co., 1969); and Robert L. Crain, *The Politics of School Desegregation* (Chicago: Aldine Publishing Co., 1967).

36. See Lewis J. Edinger, "Political Science and Political Biography: Reflections on the Study of Leadership I," *Journal of Politics* 26 (May 1964), pp. 423-39; and "Political Science and Political Biography: Reflections on the Study of Leadership II," *Journal of Politics* 26 (August 1964), pp. 648-76; also William C. Mitchell "Occupational Role Strains: The American Elective Public Official," *Administrative Science Quarterly* 3 (September 1958), pp. 210-28.

37. This process resembles the "resubordination" of the southern black after the Reconstruction era; see C. Vann Woodward, *The Strange Career of Jim Crow* (New York: Oxford University Press, 1955).

38. See Edward Greer, "Richard Hatcher and the Politics of Gary," *Social Policy* (November-December 1971), pp. 23-28; and "The Liberation of Gary, Indiana," *Trans-action* 8 (January 1971), pp. 30-39, 63.

39. In many communities a "token" minority official is an important symbol of the "progressive" outlook of the mayor and his willingness to engage in biracial leadership.

40. See *Hawkins v. Town of Shaw* 427 F. 2d 1286 (5th Cir. 1971) aff'd 461 F 2d 1171 (1972) (en banc).

41. Arend Lijphart, "Consociational Democracy," *World Politics,* 21, no. 2 (Copyright © 1969 by Princeton University Press), p. 212, Reprinted by permission of Princeton University Press.

42. Ibid., p. 216.

43. Ibid.

44. Ibid., p. 213.

45. Ibid., p. 220-21.

**Part III
Mayoral Leadership in
Three Racially Polarized
Contexts**

Cleveland: The Politics of Immobilism

Background and Structure

For nearly thirty years prior to Carl Stokes's 1967 election, Cleveland was governed by a succession of conservative, Democratic mayors of ethnic heritage. These mayors were popular in the city's white, working-class neighborhoods and won the support of Cleveland's influential newspapers by declaring their support for "good government," fiscal frugality, and nonpartisanship.[1] Because of the disinterest of these mayors in strengthening Cleveland's Democratic party, the intense rivalry between politically ambitious groups and leaders, and the political fragmentation of the city into a number of ethnic, race, class, and relgious groups, the community did not have an integrated citywide organization to facilitate mayoral leadership.[2] In Cleveland's fragmented political system, mayoral leadership consisted of the mayor's participation in various social celebrations and civic events, an occasional new public works project, and the reaffirmation of the status quo; in short, figureheadship and immobilism.

Cleveland's mayors could have provided more aggressive leadership, since the city charter provides a "strong mayor" form of government. In Cleveland's governmental system, the mayor is the only elected official in the city administration. He has an item veto over city council legislation and does not have to obtain the city council's approval to appoint department directors. However, despite this considerable formal authority, Cleveland's mayors have confronted considerable legal, jurisdictional, financial, and political constraints.

Cleveland's mayors have been hampered by their two-year term, which limits their ability to develop and activate multiyear plans and programs. In addition, some important policy areas like tax assessment and welfare are administered on a countywide rather than a citywide basis; and education is controlled by an independent, nonpartisan board of education elected on an at-large basis. Also, most city employees are insulated from mayoral influence by the government's extensive civil-service coverage. Finally, the city's declining economic base, state tax ceilings, and the low tax ideology of the city's business elite and homeowners have combined with the physical deterioration of the city and the increased social service needs of its poorer residents to limit the amount of "slack" resources available for new programs.

In addition to these legal, jurisdictional, and economic constraints, the political fragmentation of the city into separate ethnic, economic, and political groupings has produced cleavages that are manifested in important policy-making arenas like the city council and the Democratic party.[3] Cleveland's thirty-three-member city council is elected on a ward basis that quite accurately mirrors the city's ethnic and racial composition, since the settlement pattern of these groups in Cleveland has generally been homogeneous. The centrifugal force of this fragmented pattern has been so great in Cleveland that it "has determined its political superstructure. The careers of councilmen depend on appealing to separatist local interest, and these politicians reinforce the divisiveness that geographic and ethnic identity created."[4]

The separatist tendencies of Cleveland's ward-based politics has led to the institutionalization of veto privileges for councilmen who feel their neighborhoods might be adversely affected by proposals for citywide innovations. Bargaining, side payments, and the modification of proposals are often required before any mayorally initiated programs can be implemented. Over the years, cleavages between the mayor, the bureaucracies, the city council, different ethnic and racial groups, and the county and suburban governments have prevented the development of consensus behind new proposals. Disagreememts among the three principal elements of Cleveland's power structure—government, business, and the newspapers—over the economic and physical health of the city and the proper course of action to combat the city's physical and social deterioration have also contributed to political immobilism.

By the early 1960s, the sheer magnitude and urgency of local problems created demands for change. Civil-rights activism raised tensions between Cleveland's ethnic or "cosmo" (for cosmopolitan) population and the city's blacks. In response, Mayor Ralph Locher adopted a partisan posture, favoring white demands that he resist black pressure for school integration, greater participation in the local OEO-funded poverty program, and more and better city services.[5] In the summer of 1966, rioting broke out in the Hough section, one of the city's four large black ghetto areas. Locher adopted a "get tough" policy toward all black protestors, including nonviolent petitioners, offending many white liberals and blacks. By 1967, Locher had also come under heavy criticism from local newspapers and business and civic leaders. In addition to complaints about the mayor's lack of a positive response to black needs and demands, Cleveland's business community was dismayed by his lack of initiative in creating new programs for community renewal and with his inept handling of federally funded programs.[6] In 1966, Cleveland's application for a Model Cities planning grant was rejected, and federal funds for urban renewal were frozen by the Department of Housing and Urban Development.

On the eve of the 1967 Democratic primary, Ralph Locher stood on the verge of resounding defeat. The formula for mayoral leadership that had worked for his predecessors over the previous twenty-six years—frugality, honesty, boosterism, and conservatism—had failed to meet Cleveland's needs during the latter months of his administration. When the city's economic condition deteriorated during the 1960s, Locher could not adopt a new leadership style to respond effectively to the city's plight. In his analysis of Ralph Locher as a political leader, Cunningham has concluded:

For four years Ralph Locher, with Bronis Klementowicz and a few other advisors—certainly including Frank Lausche at a distance—had had their chance to create, to take risks, to organize, to seek to build Cleveland. They did none of these things. They followed a holding-action tradition which was obsolete and clearly identified themselves as routine and non-innovative. Their last year in of- fice—1967—was to be one of disintegration and defeat, with the federal govern- ment shutting off their urban renewal funds and Carl Stokes beating them at the polls. During his campaigns Stokes adroitly characterized the Lausche-Locher style as that of ''a long string of mayors who have treated the city as a trusteeship, something to be clung to and preserved, rather than developed and improved.''[7]

Electoral Politics

After 1941, the year of Frank Lausche's election to Cleveland's mayorship, politics in Cleveland became a contest between "regular" and "indepen- dent" Democrats. The independent Democrats controlled the city ad- ministration and had a base of support in the "cosmo" neighborhoods. The regular Democrats controlled the party machinery and the county govern- ment and were led by an inner circle dominated by politicians with Irish backgrounds. Contests between the two Democratic factions were mediated by the city's newspapers, especially the *Cleveland Press,* which had a large readership among Cleveland's ethnic population. The *Press* selectively endorsed Democratic candidates and through its influence on ethnic voters often provided the margin of victory in mayoral primaries. A pattern emerged in Cleveland: the *Press* would endorse a candidate in the Democratic primary, who would be opposed by a candidate endorsed by the local party. Once the newspaper's candidate won the primary and the election, the "regular" Democrats would endorse him for a second term.[8]

Because of their inability to control mayoral nominations and conse- quently city hall patronage, the "regular" Democrats were unable to build a tightly integrated organization at either the citywide or ward level. Each councilman developed his own relationship with the mayor rather than with the regular party organization and concentrated his efforts on building a personal organization within his ward. Even though the Republican party was extremely weak in Cleveland, the Democratic party was not much stronger.

As the election 1965 approached, demographic and political changes threatened to upset the city's long-established pattern of mayoral succession. While Cleveland's black population had steadily grown since World War II to comprise over one-third of the city's population, there was little increase in the influence blacks had in the political system of the city. Although there were ten blacks on the city council by 1960, there was strong resistance by the rest of the thirty-three-man body to proposals that might alleviate some of the problems of the city's black poor. Partly in anticipation of the reactions of white councilmen, and partly because of indifference, the black councilmen rarely brought up race or poverty issues. Cleveland's black politicians were simply content to maintain their own personal organizations and perquisites without being caught up in the struggle for civil rights.

By 1965 blacks were electorally very powerful in Cleveland because a vigorous Democratic voter registration drive for the 1964 presidential election increased the proportion of black voters to 40 percent of the electorate. At the same time, Locher was under heavy fire from a number of sides; the newspapers were openly critical of his administration, the Democratic party refused to endorse him, and blacks were openly antagonistic. Sensing an opportunity to replace Locher, black leaders and white liberals began searching for a candidate to challenge the mayor.

Attention began to focus on Carl B. Stokes, the first black Democrat ever to serve in the Ohio House of Representatives. Stokes had grown up in Cleveland's black ghetto, had been a high school dropout, and after a tour in the Army, graduated from law school in 1958. In 1962, after two previous unsuccessful campaigns, Stokes won a seat in the Ohio legislature, where he established himself as a savvy political independent. In 1965, Stokes calculated that he could not defeat Locher in the Democratic primary but stood a better chance of winning a four-way race as an Independent running against three white candidates: Locher, Ralph Perk, the Republican nominee, and Ralph McAllister, the conservative chairman of Cleveland's board of education, who also ran as an Independent.

Stokes's campaign strategy depended on the mathematics of Cleveland's racial composition:

The fundamental political assumptions underlying the Stokes approach were (1) a Black Democrat candidate running in a Democratic city against a White Republican opponent could count on the solid support of every Black voter who turned out; (2) a rock bottom seven in ten of the eligible Black voters would come out in this type of municipal contest with only a normal amount of organizational prodding; (3) a bedrock two in ten of the eligible White voters would vote for a Black candidate for mayor as long as he seemed more "moderate" than "militant," and this proportion might be improved a marginal amount by careful campaigning; (4) the practical danger of an exceptionally big outpouring of hostile White voters was far more real than the unrealistic dream of an exceptionally large outpouring of dedicated Black voters.[9]

But Stokes was unable to build a cohesive campaign organization. As an Independent he was denied access to Democratic ward meetings. He also was unable to enlist the aid of black ward leaders and councilmen, because they did not believe Stokes could win and feared losing their patronage from City Hall if Locher was reelected. More importantly, the 1965 Stokes campaign as an Independent lacked legitimacy; Locher was endorsed by the newspapers, and large financial contributions never materialized.

Stokes's hopes for a fairly even three-way split of the white vote between Locher, Perk, and McAllister were disappointed. Nevertheless, the final voting figures were closer than anticipated. Locher won, receiving 36.7 percent of the vote (87,858) to Stokes's 35.8 percent (84,716) with Perk and McAllister trailing far behind. Stokes received great support, as expected, from the black community, but almost no support from the white community. In short, the city divided along racial lines, with whites voting for one of the three white candidates and blacks strongly supporting Stokes.

By late spring of 1967, it was evident that Locher's popularity was at an all-time low. Stokes believed that it would be easier to defeat Locher in the primary, when a lower turnout of voters could be expected, so he decided to challenge Locher as a Democrat. Also, once elected as a Democrat, Stokes believed he could expect more help from Washington than if he were elected as an Independent. Finally, Stokes feared that the Republican nominee, Seth Taft, would withdraw from the race if Stokes declared as an Independent rather than split the white vote in the general election.[10]

Stokes began to build a campaign organization for the 1967 primary, this time with adequate funding and a full-time administrative staff. Campaign funds flowed to Stokes because Locher's ineptitude and the Hough rioting made Stokes appear an attractive alternative. Stokes explains the changes of attitude among Cleveland's civic leaders in terms of events of the previous two years:

The mourners began their search for a candidate to defeat Locher. He had been rejected, and a replacement was needed. The mood of the city was a mixture of futility and fear—futility at not being able to get the city moving, and fear of the niggers. Curiously enough, that made me obviously the most desirable candidate. I had legitimized myself as a politician in the 1965 campaign, especially in the debates, and the closeness of the election and the subsequent recount kept me in the news. I was better known than any politician in the county. The businessmen could look at my record and see that I was out there fighting for their and Jim Rhodes's pork barrel. Clearly, I was a "safe" candidate. In the backs of their minds, those white men believed that if they put me out front they would be buying off the ghetto.[11]

Stokes attacked Locher's failure to confront the city's economic stagnation and physical decay and emphasized his own ability to reconcile and reduce racial conflict in the city. In contrast, Locher campaigned on his record of honesty and fiscal frugality.

Stokes easily defeated Locher and a third candidate in the Democratic primary, receiving 52.3 percent of the vote to Locher's 43.7 percent. Stokes received approximately 16,000 votes from whites (15 percent), an increase of 12 percent over his 1965 support, and increased the cohesion of his black support from 85.4 percent in 1965 to 96.2 percent.

Immediately following his primary victory, Stokes set out to regroup Cleveland's shattered Democratic party. He was able to reunify the party to some degree and could look forward to his race with Seth Taft with confidence. He was endorsed by both major newpapers, the AFL-CIO, the Teamsters, the Democratic party, and Mayor Locher. Also, no Republican had come close to winning a mayoral election in sixteen years. Moreover, Taft's family name, associated with the anti-labor Taft-Hartley Act, was hardly an asset in heavily unionized Cleveland. Finally, Stokes had 90,000 or more black votes virtually assured, and it was expected that large numbers of lifelong white Democrats, faced with voting for a black or a Republican, would stay home.[12]

While early polls showed Stokes leading Taft by 30 percentage points, the race issue was subtly injected into the contest by both parties, and the gap between Stokes and Taft narrowed. Both Taft and Stokes took nearly identical and liberal positions on almost every important issue like law enforcement, public housing, and the curtailment of air and water pollution; but by election day, the contest for mayor was a tossup, and race was clearly the central issue.

Stokes defeated Taft by less than one percent of the total vote (129,829 to 127,328) by increasing his support within the white community (to 19.3 percent) and maintaining his strength among black voters to become the first black mayor of a major American city.

The 1969 Democratic primary and general election were critical tests of Carl Stokes's popularity and symbolic impact in Cleveland. From the time of his victory in 1967 until the 1969 election, it was generally assumed that the mayor's principal opponent would be the Republican county auditor, Ralph Perk. Perk was of Czechoslovakian descent and was extremely popular with the normally Democratic voters on the West Side. He had, for some time, been the only Republican in Cuyahoga County to consistently win countywide elections.

Before the general election, Stokes had to face Robert J. Kelly, formerly Ralph Locher's director of city services, in the Democratic primary. Kelly's primary campaign was hampered by a lack of funds and workers. The Democratic organization endorsed Stokes, but the city council president, James Stanton, and a number of West Side councilmen remained officially "neutral," tacitly supporting Kelly. Stokes conducted a leisurely primary campaign and braced himself for the upcoming campaign against Perk. Only 50 percent of Cleveland's registered voters turned out to vote in the primary, and Stokes won easily.

In the general election, Ralph Perk faced an uphill struggle. The 1970 census revealed that Cleveland's white population had declined and blacks comprised 38.5 percent of the city's population, up 3 to 4 percent over 1967 estimates. The two previous primaries and general elections revealed that election results in Cleveland were more determined by shifts in population composition than by changes in racial attitudes, and at least thirty-six precincts that were white in 1967 had turned black by 1969.[13]

Perk ran a "lusterless" race, basing his campaign on Stokes's mismanagement of the city's government. Perk charged that Stokes was leading Cleveland into financial bankruptcy, was unable to combat crime, had questionable ties with black militants, had promoted inefficiency in the administration of city services, and had inspired a lack of confidence in city government. But despite disclaimers from both sides, the race issue again dominated Cleveland politics.

In spite of efforts by some disgruntled white policemen and firemen to challenge black voters at the polls, the black turnout exceeded the white turnout by approximately 2 percent and Stokes defeated Perk by 3753 votes. Stokes had been reelected to another two-year term, but the racial division in Cleveland had been reaffirmed rather than overcome by the election.[14]

During the year and a half following the 1969 election Stokes was confronted with a series of continuing frustrations. Rising municipal service costs, racial hatred, problems with the police, newspapers and city council, and recurring rumors of city hall corruption gradually eroded Stokes's image with the city's white liberal and business communities. After Stokes supported the organization of the all-black 21st Congressional District Caucus that split from the regular Democratic party, there was speculation that he would make it into a third political party and run for reelection in 1971 against white Republican and Democratic candidates. But Stokes calculated that he could not win another election against Perk in 1971 and announced his intention not to seek a third term. The mayor pledged his support to a black Independent, Arnold R. Pinckney, his former campaign director and president of Cleveland's board of education.

Before formally endorsing Pinckney, Stokes supported a white liberal, James Carney, in the Democratic primary in a effort to thwart conservative city council president Anthony Garofoli's bid for the Democratic nomination. Because of Stokes's support, a surprisingly large number of blacks turned out to vote in the Democratic primary, and Carney upset Garofoli.

Stokes then switched his endorsement to Pinckney. But Stokes's overt attempt to manipulate the black vote infuriated whites and alienated blacks. Pinckney, who lacked an independent base of support and charisma, ran far behind Stokes's 1967 and 1969 totals in both black and white wards and lost.[15] Perk drew 12,579 votes more than Pinckney, who drew only 77 percent of the black vote, 21 percent going to Carney. The defeat of Stokes's candidate and the adverse reaction to his tactical switch cost him considerable national and local prestige and adversely affected his opportunities for continued political prominence in Cleveland.

Policy Politics and Leadership Structure

In the early months of his administration, Stokes seemed unable to create a program that would mobilize community influentials and symbolize change. He scored some early victories with the lifting of the freeze on federal funds for urban renewal and received a series of federal grants for housing and job training. But the mayor was unable to activate the city's business community to contribute more than token vocal support for his administration.[16] Despite Stokes's personal charisma and promotional activism, the city's long history of mayoral nonleadership and the inexperience of the mayor's new staff created too much inertia for Stokes to overcome in the first few months following his inauguration.[17]

Just as Stokes appeared to be faltering in his attempt to mobilize Cleveland, Martin Luther King was assassinated in Memphis and rioting erupted in black ghettos all over the country. Cleveland was exceptionally calm because Stokes personally visited the inner city to persuade militants not to riot. His success at preventing rioting impressed many of the city's civic leaders and led to offers to help Stokes improve living conditions in Cleveland. Shortly afterwards, Stokes, capitalizing on his prestige, proposed a new multifaceted community development program called "Cleveland: NOW!" that was designed to use federal, foundation, and privately contributed funds to improve housing, recreation facilities, and employment opportunities in the inner city.[18]

"Cleveland: NOW!" became the slogan and symbolic nexus of Stokes's public relations program.[19] Through the program the mayor sought to involve a wide range of Clevelanders, particularly the business community, and to build an executive-centered coalition. Stokes immediately won the support of the two major newspapers, and the "Cleveland: NOW!" campaign attracted the enthusiastic involvement and financial support of a number of business leaders. For the first time in many years, a Cleveland mayor was able to mobilize community influentials behind an innovative, large-scale program. Cleveland's business community even pledged $11 million to Stokes's campaign. Only the city's white ethnic communities remained skeptical of Stokes's ability to provide communitywide leadership.

After a short period of euphoric optimism in 1968, the "Cleveland: NOW!" campaign and Stokes's incipient coalition began to disintegrate. A business recession and the reduced threat of ghetto rioting dampened the spirit of private contributors; actual contributions to the fund-raising drive barely exceeded half the $11 million pledged.[20] But perhaps the most important single cause of the program's loss of vitality was a gunfight between police and a group of black nationalists in the city's Glenville neighborhood. After the gunfight, rioting broke out, and Stokes, in an effort to minimize further violence, ordered the withdrawal of white police officers from the area, leaving the area patrolled only by black officers. The white police officers were furious, and the controversy intensified when it was alleged that the guns used by the black nationalists were purchased with funds from a "Cleveland: NOW!" grant.[21] Stokes's opponents charged the mayor with failing to suppress the city's black militants. Donations for "Cleveland: NOW!" slowed to a trickle. By the mayoral campaign of 1969, "Cleveland: NOW!" was little more than a memory and Stokes's embryonic executive-centered coalition had disintegrated.

From the beginning of his administration, Stokes attempted to generate political resources from the previously unexploited powers of Cleveland's mayoralty. He quickly assumed control over some aspects of city services that had traditionally been left to the authority of department heads. By assuming the position of the person to see about such routine city services as street repairing and recreational facilities, Stokes attempted to exert greater influence over the city council than had his predecessors. The city council, however, reflecting the grass-roots orientation of individual councilmen, polarized along racial lines like the rest of the city, denying Stokes the influence he sought over council policy making.

The Cleveland city council was dominated by Democrats; twenty-seven of its thirty-three members were Democrats in 1970. But party affiliation was less important than race in council voting. During Stokes's two terms, the council was divided along racial lines into two extremely cohesive blocs.[22] One bloc was led by the city council president and was composed of sixteen white and three black councilmen. The other bloc was loyal to Stokes and was composed of eleven black and three white councilmen. Of the six councilmen who crossed racial lines, two white councilmen were elected from predominantly black wards and the third represented a ward that was rapidly turning into a black majority. The voting records of the three black Democrats who supported the anti-Stokes leadership of council presidents James Stanton (until September 1970) and Anthony Garofoli (from September 1970 until November 1971) were motivated by their ambition for countywide office and "their attitudes which tended to be similar to those of the council leadership."[23]

Because he could not command the loyalty of a majority of the city council, "Stokes's impact on controversial policies was limited primarily to the use of threat to use the mayoral veto."[24] So that the council leadership could not mobilize the needed twenty-two votes to override mayoral vetoes, Stokes encouraged the development of the "rebel caucus" of councilmen who opposed Stanton and Garofoli.[25] The caucus became Stokes's principal weapon in the council and an arm of the 21st District Caucus. While Stokes could block new legislation by vetoing it, he did not control a majority of the council and could not successfully propose new programs opposed by the council leadership.

Stokes also found that many of the problems which he attributed in his campaign to the ineptitude of the Locher administration could not be easily solved. The money he alleged to be "hidden" in Locher's budgets that would allow him to avoid tax increases simply could not be found. Even when tax referendums were passed to raise additional revenue, inflation and increased salary demands from civil servants absorbed almost all of the slack. Throughout his four-year term, with the exception of the few euphoric months of "Cleveland: NOW!" and the overlap with the final months of the Johnson administration in Washington, Stokes never had sufficient resources to appreciably alter Cleveland's growing physical and social decay.

The most glaring and continuous failure of Carl Stokes's leadership efforts were his relationships with Cleveland's police department. Throughout his two terms, mayoral-police relations produced a series of frustrations for the mayor that stifled his entire program. Relations between Cleveland's blacks and police were never tranquil. Blacks were vastly underrepresented on Cleveland's police force, and continuous charges of police brutality, poor service, and racism made by black leaders were ignored by police leadership. A clash between Stokes and the police was an inevitable outgrowth of long years of hostility and resentment toward police practices by the black community.

Stokes's problems with Cleveland's police surfaced even before his election in 1967 when he announced his intention to fire the police chief at a meeting of the Fraternal Order of Police. After his election, Stokes and the police fought over salaries, the assignment of policemen with office jobs to patrol duty, and the administration of civil-service entrance exams. The Glenville shoot-out further exacerbated the conflict between the mayor and the police force. White groups were organized to back the police force in civil suits, disciplinary actions, and in their demands for heavy weaponry to fight black militants. Anti-Stokes partisans even made efforts to link the mayor to the deaths of the three policemen killed during the Glenville shoot-out.

Stokes responded with rhetoric about the importance of "law and order" and even proposed a prolonged "war on crime." But no matter how hard Stokes tried to win the confidence of the police force, the pattern of antagonsim was already firmly established. For example, during the 1969 election, over two hundred policemen and one hundred firemen, dressed in civilian clothing, appeared as vote challengers and witnessess at polling places in black precincts to slow the voting process.

The tension between the mayor and the police was reflected in the high turnover of police chiefs and safety directors during Stokes's administration. One appointee was accused of taking bribes in Detroit and never assumed the police chief's duties. The resignation of another, retired Air Force lieutenant general, Benjamin O. Davis, marked a low ebb in Stokes's credibility. After less then six months in office, Davis resigned, charging that Stokes and members of his administration provided support and comfort to "the enemies of law enforcement."[26]

By early 1969, with the prospects for a biracial executive-centered coalition fading, Stokes began to seek a new leadership strategy. For a short time, prior to the 1969 election, Stokes adopted a bystander strategy toward racial issues. For example, during the summer of 1969, a coalition of black groups led by black nationalists attempted to enforce a boycott of McDonald's restaurants in an effort to force the firm to sell its franchises in the black community to black owners. Stokes remained aloof from the controversy for over four months. Only on the eve of the election, after receiving a great deal of criticism for his neutrality stance, did he seize the initiative and help negotiate a settlement. Stokes's neutrality during the McDonald's controversy gained him few white allies, and shortly after the 1969 election, he began to adopt a more partisan leadership style.

During Stokes's second term, he spoke out more forcefully for black political interests. At the local level, Stokes helped invigorate the 21st Congressional District Caucus as an alternative to the regular Democratic party in order to organize the black community and coordinate the efforts of black politicians. He also fought to end job discrimination in local unions by threatening to withhold construction contracts from those unions with discriminatory practices. In addition, Stokes criticized police and newspaper racism, fought the city council for integrated scattered-site public housing in black and white middle-class neighborhoods, fought losing battles for tax increases, and withdrew the city from the Northeast Ohio Area Coordinating Agency (NOACA). At the national level, Stokes became an active lobbyist for revenue sharing and a spokesman for black economic development and political power. This combination of local partisanship and national involvement strengthened Stokes's position as a black leader, but alienated many Cleveland whites who had supported him in the past. Stokes summarizes his second term as "almost total war between the mayor and the Council, between the mayor and the newspapers, between the mayor and everyone."[27]

Achievements and Failures

Stokes left Cleveland's mayoralty with a number of achievements. He was able to generate a substantial amount of federal financial support for a variety of redevelopment projects involving new housing, recreation, and job-training programs. According to Stokes:

Housing was one of my true and lasting achievements. When I took office there had been no new public housing built in five years and there was none under contract. When I left office four years later we had 5,496 units of low and moderate income housing at a cost of more than $102 million. No city in the country had a record like that. A project that vigorous was bound to be highly visible, and, just as naturally, to cause a good deal of opposition in neighborhoods where no low-income housing had gone before. This was especially true in middle-class neighborhoods where we erected housing for the poor. The opposition was not solely a racial matter; it also reflected class hostility. We faced the same bright-red angers in Lee-Seville, a middle-class black neighborhood, as we did in the white southwest side of Cleveland. But, although we were blocked in some cases—Lee-Seville was the most dramatic—we were successful in the overall project.[28]

In addition to these physical improvements, Stokes could also take credit for some symbolic changes. First, he was instrumental in alerting national policy-makers to Cleveland's problems. Second, a number of highly talented younger administrators were brought into the city government, and a number of civic and business leaders became involved for the first time in efforts to solve the city's problems. Finally, Stokes provided Cleveland's blacks with a sense of political efficacy, a locally accessible national leader, and an inspirational symbol of black achievement.

On the negative side, Stokes left Cleveland $26 million in debt because a Stokes-supported proposal to increase the city's income tax was defeated in a November 1970 referendum. The financial squeeze forced Stokes to fire over fifteen hundred city employees including garbage collectors, housing inspectors, policemen, and health officers. Also, in January 1971, the Department of Housing and Urban Development temporarily froze Cleveland's federal funds for urban renewal, public housing, housing demolition, and rent supplements, because the city council refused to approve an agreement to build low-and moderate-income public housing in white neighborhoods.[29] But, the mayor's greatest frustration came from his inability to reform Cleveland's police department. The department was able to withstand a succession of Stokes-appointed safety directors and police chiefs to remain almost totally independent of mayoral influence throughout Stokes's four years in office.[30] Finally, Pinckney's defeat ended black control of city hall. The failure to institutionalize black mayoral leadership in Cleveland and Mayor Perk's commitment to adopt a leadership style similar to those mayors of the pre-Stokes era meant that the prospects for an executive-centered biracial coalition fostering continued development of the black community would be minimal.

In summary, Carl Stokes's two terms as Cleveland's mayor demonstrate the fragile position of a black leader in a racially polarized, white-dominated community. His mayoralty also demonstrates the limitations of the executive-centered coalition model as a leadership strategy in a polarized community. For a short time in his first term, Stokes was able to *centralize* politics in the mayoralty, *mobilize* and *integrate* some important community interest groups and institutions, and activate some *innovative* changes. Over time, the community's racial polarization caused the disintegration of his nascent executive-centered coalition and led him to adopt a more racially partisan leadership strategy. From a pluralist perspective, Stokes's inability to institutionalize an executive-centered coalition would be an indicator of the ineffectiveness of his leadership. However, his use of mayoral influence to benefit the black community and to mobilize and integrate the city's blacks into an institutionalized coalition—the 21st Congressional District Caucus—would give him a much higher score on a scale constructed from a conflict perspective.

Notes

1. For a discussion of the frugality of some of Stokes's predecessors, see John E. Jackson, "Politics and the Budgetary Process," *Social Science Research* 1 (April 1972), pp. 35-60.

2. See Matthew Holden, Jr., "Decision-Making on a Metropolitan Government Proposal," in Scott Greer et al., eds. *The New Urbanization* (New York: St. Martin's Press, 1968), p. 318.

3. See David Rogers, *The Management of Big Cities: Interest Groups and Social Change Strategies* (Beverly Hills, Calif.: Sage Publications, 1971), pp. 117-19.

4. Ibid., p. 114.

5. See Kenneth G. Weinberg, *Black Victory: Carl Stokes and the Winning of Cleveland* (Chicago: Quadrangle Books, 1968); and Louis H. Masotti and Jerome R. Corsi, *Shoot-Out in Cleveland: Black Militants and the Police, July 23, 1968* (New York: Frederick A. Praeger, 1969).

6. See Jeffrey K. Hadden, Louis H. Masotti, and Victor Thiessen, "The Making of the Negro Mayors 1967," *Trans-action* 5 (January-February 1968), pp. 21-30; Ruth Fisher, "Why Hough Got Tough—the Real Agitators," *New Republic* 155 (September 10, 1966), pp. 9-10; Roldo S. Bartimole and Murray Gruber, "Cleveland: Recipe for Violence," *Nation* 204 (June 26, 1967), pp. 814-17; Walter Williams, "Cleveland's Crisis Ghetto," *Trans-action* 4 (September, 1967), pp. 33-42; Walt Anderson, *Campaigns: Cases in Political Conflict* (Pacific Palisades, Calif.: Goodyear Publishing Co., 1970), p. 217; and James M. Naughton, "In Cleveland and Boston, the Issue is Race," *New York Times Magazine,* 5 November 1967, p. 30.

7. James V. Cunningham, *Urban Leadership in the Sixties* (Cambridge, Mass.: Schenkman Publishing Co., 1970), p. 33.

8. See Holden, "Decision-Making on a Metropolitan Government Proposal," pp. 318-19. According to Holden:

The *Press* had had a policy for the past quarter century of backing any important politician opposed to the regular Democrats. Most of the time since the *Press* could not actually make Democrats vote Republican this meant the *Press* had to find acceptable Democrats (i.e., Democrats who were important enough to merit the marginal support of the *Press* but weak enough so that the marginal support of the *Press* would be essential). This usually meant cosmopolitans: in 1968 it meant the mayor.

9. Penn Kimball, *The Disconnected* (New York: Columbia University Press, 1972), pp. 153-54.

10. See Weinberg, *Black Victory,* pp. 167-75.

11. Carl B. Stokes, *Promises of Power: A Political Autobiography* (New York: Simon and Schuster, 1973), p. 96. Copyright © 1973 by Carl B. Stokes, Reprinted by permission of Simon and Schuster.

12. See Hadden, Masotti, and Thiessen, "The Making of the Negro Mayors 1967," p. 24.

13. See Samuel Lubell, "Stokes is Losing Support from West Side Whites," *Cleveland Press* 15 September 1969, pp. A1 and A4; "Negro Shift Aids Stokes Vote Total," *Cleveland Press* 2 October 1969, p. B5; and *The Hidden Crisis in American Politics* (New York: W.W. Norton & Co., 1970), pp. 103-4.

14. The only wards without lopsided tallies were racially changing neighborhoods on the East Side, and in these wards members of each racial groups voted their prejudices even more heavily than in the rest of the city. Even though Stokes received an estimated 22 percent of the West Side vote, voters in a number of ethnic precincts supported Perk more heavily than they had supported Taft in 1967.

15. See Stokes, *Promises of Power,* p. 247.

16. See James M. Naughton, "Mayor Stokes: The First Hundred Days," *New York Times Magazine,* 25 February 1968, p. 27; "Carl Stokes' First Year as Mayor," *Cleveland Plain Dealer* 17 November 1968; Adele Zeidman Silver, "Cleveland's 100 Days: The Education of Carl Stokes," *Nation* 206 (March 18, 1968), pp. 379-80; and Morton Kondracke, "No Miracles, Some Progress," *Progressive* 32 (May 1968), p. 37.

17. See Stokes, *Promises of Power,* pp. 108-30.

18. See Timothy Ambruster, " 'Cleveland Now:' One City's Program for Change," *Current History* 54 (December 1968), pp. 357-61.

19. See Stokes, *Promises of Power,* p. 130. Stokes admits: "There was a lot about the program that was pure public relations. Everything positive that happened over that eighteen-month period was announced as a Cleveland: NOW! achievement. Obviously that was not always true."

20. See Rogers, *The Management of Big Cities,* p. 123.

21. See Donn Pearce, "Oh, that Ahmed. Poor, Poor Ahmed. They're Going to Fry His Black Skinny Ass," *Esquire* 73 (March 1970), pp. 128-35; John Skow, "Cleveland: The Flicker of Fear," *Saturday Evening Post* 241 (September 7, 1968), pp. 23-27; Terence Sheridan, "Black and Blue in Cleveland," *Nation* 211 (July 20, 1970), pp. 48-50; and Masotti and Corsi, *Shoot-Out in Cleveland.*

22. See Kenneth R. Green, "Overt Issue Conflict on the Cleveland City Council, 1970-1971," a paper delivered at the Sixty-sixth Annual Meeting of the American Political Science Association, New Orleans, Louisiana, September 4-8, 1973.

23. Ibid.

24. Ibid.

25. See Stokes, *Promises of Power,* pp. 131-45.

26. Ibid., p. 200.

27. Ibid., p. 244. Copyright © 1973 by Carl B. Stokes. Reprinted by permission of Simon and Schuster.

28. Ibid., p. 124. Copyright © 1973 by Carl B. Stokes. Reprinted by permission of Simon and Schuster.

29. See Francis Ward, "Cleveland: Bleak Prospects," *Washington Post,* 7 May 1971, p. B2.

30. See Stokes, *Promises of Power,* p. 146.

5

Gary: The Politics of Racial Partisanship

Background and Structure

During the sixty years prior to Richard Hatcher's 1967 election, Gary's politics were dominated by corrupt and conservative machine politicians. After two decades of Republican rule, a highly centralized Democratic machine emerged during the 1930s to control elections and policy making for the next thirty-five years. During this period corruption dominated local decision making; one mayor was sent to jail, another was indicted, and two or three others were alleged to have made illegal fortunes while in office. To maintain its dominance of local politics, the Democratic machine practiced a conscious policy of nondecision making, avoiding and suppressing issues and proposals that would endanger any important element in its coalition; issues that might exacerbate racial tensions, infringe on the perogatives of the US Steel Corporation, or interfere with the operations of organized crime.[1] Within Gary's political system the mayor stood at or near the center, protecting the status quo, rewarding friends, and punishing enemies of the machine. In short, Gary's executive-centered coalition was a conservative, broker-oriented structure maintained by the trading of votes and money for power and privileges.

While Gary's politics were integrated by the considerable informal powers of the Democratic machine, they were centralized by the formal powers of the mayor. Gary has a "strong mayor" form of government. The mayor has wide and extensive powers of appointment, an executive veto, a four-year term, and over one thousand patronage appointments, which include sole or controlling membership on almost all the city's major boards and agencies. He can run for reelection and submits an executive budget the city council can only amend downward (except for the salaries of firemen and policemen). The mayor also appoints the city's three chief executive officers (the city controller, the city attorney, and the city engineer) who also make up Gary's board of public works and safety.

Despite these substantial powers, nondecision making in Gary was reinforced by some jurisidictional constraints that limited the local government's discretion. Mayors could attribute their inaction to their lack of jurisdiction over some important functions like welfare, tax assessment, and tax collection, which are controlled by the county and township governments that overlap and subdivide Gary. Inertia is also built into local decisionmaking by the staggered terms of members of the independent police, fire, health, park, and redevelopment commissions. It has been estimated that it would take seven years before a newly elected mayor's appointment power would guarantee him control of these vital commissions.[2]

Gary's Democratic machine maintained control of city politics well after similar machines had disintegrated in other cities. The machine effectively balanced the needs of the city's five major interest groups—white ethnics, blacks, unions, business (especially US Steel), and organized crime—in a smoothly functioning, but conservative coalition.[3] During the late 1950s and early 1960s, however, a number of changes caused the machine's coalition to become inherently unstable.

During this period, Gary's unionized workers enjoyed a period of relative prosperity. Many of the city's white residents were able to become homeowners for the first time. Their prosperity devalued the importance of the machine's patronage, and many of the new homeowners adopted an anticorruption, "good government" ideology. At the same time, Gary's black community grew enormously, comprising almost 50 percent of the population by 1965. The less prosperous black community was more attracted to the machine's patronage, favors, and influence than the white community.[4] For three decades, Gary's black politicians delivered the black vote and suppressed racial issues that might embarrass or weaken the machine. By the mid-1960s, however, black voters comprised the only faction of the machine's coalition that it could count on for disciplined voting support. Because of its dependence on black voters, the machine was forced to adjust to increased demands that it distribute more rewards to the black community. But the conservatism of the machine, its corruption, and the changing racial composition of the city eventually undermined its capability to retain control of the city. During the mid-sixties, the conservative, white leadership of the machine tried but simply could not adapt to the new demands of Gary's blacks or confront obvious pollution and physical decay problems that only strengthened demands for change.

Electoral Politics

The election of 1963 highlighted the striking lack of support for the machine in the white community and the voting power of Gary's blacks. Instead of the single candidate for the mayoral nomination one might expect in a machine-controlled city, there were five strong candidates. The machine chose to support A. Martin Katz, a city court judge, because he was the only major party regular with electoral experience who had not been intimately associated with the corruption of the previous administration and had a reputation as a liberal in the black community. Katz won the primary by less than three thousand votes, but he failed to carry a single white precinct in either the primary or the general election, winning because of black voting support.

The 1963 election also witnessed the election of Richard Hatcher to Gary's city council. For the 1963 election, the machine was without an adequate black candidate for one of the three councilmen-at-large positions it had traditionally reserved for a black candidate. The incumbent had been involved in a scandal and was unacceptable to both the black and white communities. Hatcher was suggested for the nomination because he had served as a deputy county prosecutor, and it was assumed he would cooperate with the machine because every other black politician who had ever been elected to the city council had been cooperative. The machine never openly endorsed Hatcher, but its leadership opposed one of Hatcher's black primary opponents, a civil-rights activist.

Upon Hatcher's election to the council, he immediately established himself as a new kind of black politician. He joined the "economy bloc" on the council, championed civil-rights causes, and with Katz's support was elected president of the city council.

The emergence of open occupancy as a crucial issue in Gary city politics drove a deep wedge between Hatcher and the rest of the city council. Hatcher became personally identified with an ordinance for open occupancy that was voted on a number of times in 1964. The issue became the most salient test of the machine's commitment to the black community. Katz began to pressure councilmen to support the bill, and eventually it passed. But although the bill could not have passed without Katz's support, the victory was considered to be Hatcher's in the black community. Hatcher's reputation and popularity soared with the passage of the bill. He became the obvious choice for the first black attempt to capture the mayoralty.

By 1967 the city was in an advanced state of physical and spiritual decay. Neither local business nor US Steel seemed interested in taking the initative in turing the tide on the city's decline. The white middle class and potential young white leaders were moving to the suburbs. Because the city's electorate was nearly half black and the majority of the Democratic party was black, Gary's young aggressive black professionals and white middle-class liberals sensed an opportunity to do something about the city's political and ecological decay.

Although there was some talk about the machine running a black candidate for mayor in 1967, Katz thought he should have an opportunity for reelection. Katz's adminstration can be characterized as a transitional attempt to adjust city policy to meet black demands for change. Under his administration, every city commission was integrated for the first time, blacks were appointed as corporation counsel, superintendent of sanitation, deputy controller, assistant director of general services, and two blacks were promoted to assistant fire chief. Katz also appointed thirty-two black firemen, as many as had been appointed in the entire sixty-year history of Gary.[5] In addition, Katz made application for, and received, some federal aid for urban renewal, public housing, and OEO programs.

But though Gary was a predominantly black city, the most important jobs in city government were still denied to blacks. Of the twenty-six departments of the city government, only two were headed by black people. Of Gary's four state representatives, none were black. Of the nine-men city council, only three were black. Both judges serving Gary were white. According to the Indiana Civil Rights Commission, only 28 percent of the twenty thousand city jobs were held by blacks. Hatcher used these figures to show how black people were underrepresented in Gary's government. He also claimed that the city was in danger of losing its federal support and would be denied additional funds because of the gross mismanagement and corruption in city hall.[6]

Hatcher's support in the primary came from a wide cross-section of the black community as well as from some whites determined to defeat the machine. Gary's Democratic machine was ripped apart as blacks defected to Hatcher and whites to Bernard Konrady, a white conservative reformer. The results of the 1967 Democratic primary were: Hatcher, 20,272; Katz, 17,910; and Konrady, 13,133. Voting was primarily along racial lines. Hatcher received 75 percent of the black vote, Katz 24 percent, and Konrady 1 percent. Konrady received 46 percent of the white votes, Katz 45 percent, and Hatcher 7 percent.[7]

At first it was assumed that by capturing the Democratic nomination Hatcher was assured of victory in the general election, since Gary was predominantly Democratic and there was little fear of a total white abandonment of the Democratic ticket. But Hatcher refused to accede to Lake County democratic chairman John G. Krupa's demands for control over certain appointments; and the machine endorsed Joseph B. Radigan, Hatcher's Republican opponent. The Hatcher-Krupa conflict polarized the city along racial lines and tension escalated further after the Justice Department ruled in favor of Hatcher, charging that the election board had acted illegally when it invalidated the registration of 5,000 black voters and added nonexistent whites. On election eve, the fear of violence prompted the Governor to call up 4,000 National Guardsmen.[8]

Almost 75 percent of Gary's registered voters turned out to vote in the general election and Hatcher defeated Radigan by some 1,400 votes, 39,330 to 37,941. He was able to win by receiving almost 93 percent of the black vote, about 17 percent of the white vote, and 55 to 60 percent of the Latin-American vote. He received between 4000 and 6000 white votes because of loyalty to the Democratic party and white liberal opposition to the machine.

As the 1971 election approached, some political observers thought they had found a potential source of weakness in the mayor's failure to build his own precinct-level organization. (A year before the election Hatcher had failed to win the post of Democratic city chairman in a vote of Democratic precinct captains.) The machine's control of the precinct captains and its nomination of a black primary opponent were considered threats to Hatcher's hold on black voters. However, Hatcher easily defeated Dr. Alexander Williams, Lake County coroner, the machine's black candidate, by 13,908 votes in the primary and soundly defeated a white Republican by over fifty thousand votes in the general election. The magnitude of Hatcher's victories and the mobilization of over three thousand volunteers for the 1971 campaign shattered the myth of the mayor's electoral vulnerablity.

In the 1971 election, some of Hatcher's opponents on the city council retired and five black council candidates who pledged to support the mayor were elected. The Gary Democratic party endorsed Hatcher in the 1971 general election, an indication that the machine was prepared to acknowledge Hatcher's popularity and accept him as a fact of political life in Gary.[9]

Policy Politics and Leadership Structure

To understand policy politics in Gary, it is helpful to view Richard Hatcher as a new type of reform mayor. In his inaugural address, the new mayor espoused the "good government" creed of the metropolitan reform movement, but added a new dimension: the responsibility of local government to improve the living conditions of the black poor.

Let it be known that as of this moment, there are some who are no longer welcome in Gary, Indiana. Those who have made a profession of violating our laws—are no longer welcome. . . . Those who would bribe our policemen and other public officials and those public officials who accept bribes are no longer welcome. . . .

A special word to my brothers and sisters who because of circumstances beyond your control, find yourselves locked into miserable slums, without enough food to eat, inadequate clothing for your children and no hope for tomorrow. It is a primary goal of this administration to make your life better. . . .

. . . for we seek a high and beautiful new plateau—a new plateau of economy and efficiency in government, a new plateau of progress in government: a new plateau where every man, democrat and republican, rich and poor, Jew and Gentile, black and white, shall live in peace and dignity.[10]

Consistent with this theme, Hatcher rejected the machine's offer of support in exchange for veto privileges over certain key appointments and policy areas. The mayor believed that the concessions demanded by the machine would prevent him from achieving meaningful change in Gary. The machine responded by attacking Hatcher, accusing him of being a "communist" and a "black racist." The mayor and members of his staff replied with charges that the leaders of the machine were "crooks" and "racketeers."[11]

Hatcher's dedication to honest government, his reform ideals, and his attacks on crime and vice cast an aura of respectability around city government that it had not enjoyed in years. But his insistence on integrity in government created some major problems for the mayor. Hatcher's opposition to "payoffs," "kickbacks," and "payrollers," meant that some city councilmen and precinct captains, who profited under former administrations, would be deprived of sizable incomes. Naturally, they vowed to disrupt and block as many of the mayor's programs as they could.

In addition to Hatcher's reform ideology, his commitment to black political and economic development further complicated his performance as Gary's mayor. The two early slogans for his administration—"Let's get ourselves together" and "One Gary"—met with extreme cynicism from many of the city's white residents, who felt they were hollow slogans to mask Hatcher's intention to favor blacks in jobs, housing, and services. Hatcher often maintained that his favoritism toward blacks was a short-run adjustment of city services that was necessary to rectify imbalances that had developed over the years, but that over the long run he supported greater understanding and equality between the races. Although he often articulated a moderate racial stance, many whites firmly believed that Hatcher was a black supremacist. One example of white unhappiness with Hatcher's mayorship was the unsuccessful attempt of some residents of Gary's southern section, Glen Park, to disannex from the city. They were finally dissuaded by the enormous cost of building facilities and buying equipment for a new city without the tax revenues from US Steel.[12]

Hatcher's more militant statements and activities heightened white antagonism but a number of black activists were also hostile toward him for different reasons. They believed that once Hatcher was elected mayor, graft, patronage, and power would be funneled exclusively into the black community. But the mayor's commitment to honest and effective city government resulted in a crackdown on organized crime run by both black and white racketeers, the elimination of graft, the appointment of some white professionals to top-level administrative positions, and some cooperation with the white business, labor, and professional establishments.

The conflict between municipal reform and black advancement goals often exposed Hatcher to criticism from either blacks or whites who supported one but not the other of his two change goals. Normally, a mayor with a greatly expanded budget and massive outside financial resources should be expected to be more influential than his predecessors but because Hatcher was committed to opposing the policies of previous administrations and reinstating the privileges and immunities granted to special interests, he was unable to gain the support of a number of powerful groups in the community.

The focal point and most vociferous source of disenchantment with the Hatcher administration was Gary's city council. Traditionally, the city council worked closely with Gary's mayor; its members were given a good deal of influence over appointments and, it is alleged, contracts and law enforcement. The councilmen were so loyal to previous mayors that they were often accused of being "rubber stamps." Hatcher broke with tradition, refusing to grant privileges that some councilmen thought were perquisites of their position and alienated a number of councilmen in the process.

Voting on the city council between 1967 and 1971 was very complicated because three of the five councilmen who were aligned with the Lake County Democratic organization were black, and a fourth councilman was a Latin-American. Every councilman felt the cross pressures of racial issues and reform politics. While most of the business that came before the council concerned routine traditional city services, such matters as budget ordinances, zoning changes, salaries, new personnel, and the conduct of some city departments caused heated controversies and splits within the council.

Mayor Hatcher could count on no "rubber stamps" on Gary's 1967-71 city council. In fact, there was often open hostility between the mayor and some councilmen. Although he occasionally consulted with individual councilmen on appointments and ordinances, many councilmen felt they were neglected and their advice ignored. A close Hatcher aide offered an explanation as to why he believed the mayor ignored some of the councilmen:

Some of the councilmen tried to trade their votes on important bills for a partial return to the past. They wanted to get control over some jobs, contracts, and patronage. Two or three of them even tried to get the rackets—numbers and prostitution—reinstalled in their districts. They talked a lot about communication gaps, but what really existed was a corruption gap.[13]

In spite of the antagonism many councilmen felt toward the mayor, their unwillingness to cooperate with Hatcher did not operate to his disadvantage as often as one might expect. On most nonracial issues, Hatcher could depend on the support of two or three white councilmen who were independent of the machine and could sometimes get support from one or two other councilmen. On issues that clearly benefitted the city's blacks, such as public housing applications, federal grant applications for job training, and Model Cities funds, Hatcher could generally depend on pressure from the black commumity to influence black councilmen to support his programs. Finally, on "law and order" issues, like increasing the size of the police force to combat street crime, the mayor had the support of virtually the entire council. In short, despite hostilities, Hatcher managed to gain the support of individual councilmen when his programs coincided with their interests.

Nevertheless, Hatcher attempted to avoid council scrutiny over his programs as much as possible and used some very ingenious tactics to circumvent council authority. An example of the mayor's strategy to avoid the council was in the area of public housing construction. Because the council had control over zoning changes and had been reluctant to grant zoning changes, the Gary housing commission adopted a policy of constructing small, "turn-key" housing developments that met the zoning standards already prescribed for a neighborhood. In this manner a large number of public housing units were built without the council scrutinizing appeals for rezoning.

The single most important institution in Gary is the US Steel Corporation. Since it is by far the city's major taxpayer, the firm's willingness to cooperate with Hatcher was a crucial factor in his efforts to improve the city. Hatcher hoped to get US Steel reinvolved in the city's problems after nearly forty years of disinterest, while at the same time removing its privileged status. He was somewhat successful at mobilizing the company to help the city, but less successful at raising its tax assessment, changing the method by which the company paid for building permits for plant expansion, or modifying its effluent discharge policies.[14]

Roughly 46 percent of Gary's property tax is paid by US Steel. Without a major tax reassessment of US Steel or an increase in other forms of taxable construction, which is unlikely, Gary's future financial situation appears bleak. The 1970 school budget was drastically cut because it called for a tax levy in excess of the Indiana state maximum. Gary's firemen, teachers, and general service workers struck for higher wages and the police department experienced a slowdown over wages. Even bond issues for service equipment met resistance. Gary still depends on a property tax for 80 percent of its municipal revenue, and despite US Steel's cooperation in other areas, it is unlikely the company will readily cooperate with any reassessment program.

In spite of a rancorous political environment, Hatcher continued to seek a means of building communitywide support for his administration. However, he was unable to gain the full support of Gary's leading newspaper, the *Gary Post-Tribune*, to attract the support of most of the white community, or to persuade Gary's business community to give anything more than token support for his programs. With little consensus existing between the mayor and local business, labor, and political leaders (including a number of black politicians allied with the Democratic machine), there was little prospect for biracial municipal reform efforts or for an internally financed citywide development program. Instead of relying on local resources, Hatcher sought funds and support from the federal government, private foundations, national political leaders, and the national media.[15]

Given the mayor's goals—municipal reform and black development—it is unlikely that Hatcher could have built an innovative leadership structure from the interests that prevailed during former administrations. But, by enlisting the aid of the federal government and private foundations, Hatcher was able to avoid political compromises with local politicians who would have thwarted his programs if local resources were his only source of funds. In short, Hatcher's "new convergence of power" did not include many of the interests traditionally associated with political power in Gary. Instead, Hatcher built a new coalition of federal agencies, foundations, professional administrators, and the city's black masses that was effective in making changes without incorporating local interests which were formally politically significant.

Achievements and Failures

A judgment about the effectiveness of a mayor must consider both his symbolic impact and substantive achievements. In Gary, like Cleveland, the symbolic output of local government was particularly significant because the mayor was black, and race affected perceptions of Richard Hatcher's substantive accomplishments.

In the first two years of Hatcher's mayorship, the most dramatic change in Gary came from the interest of the Johnson administration in giving Hatcher a boost. Most of the support continued during the first few years of the Nixon administration, because Hatcher and his aides were able to effectively argue that Gary could serve as an excellent laboratory for social experimentation.[16]

Almost $30 million of federal aid was funneled into Gary in the first two years of Hatcher's adminstration, more than the city had attracted in its entire history. In all, it has been estimated that $150 million of federal funds were committed to the city during Hatcher's first five years in office. Much of the money spent in the first two years was for programs the Katz administration had applied for, but which had been either frozen or not appropriated prior to Hatcher's election. Some of the federal funds undoubtedly would have come to Gary even if Hatcher had been defeated, but

not nearly as quickly or in such large amounts as occurred after his victory.
    The new funds dramatically altered the pace of change in Gary:

For a while people were going around saying Gary was lucky to be in such bad
shape; it would get so much help that it would be a model of what could be done to
regenerate cities. And for a while it looked as if the experiment might just work.
The level of administrative competence was nothing to boast of, but things did
happen, and without the traditional payoffs and graft. A good deal of excellent
low-income housing was built; 4,500 new units in five years. Education and health
programs were started. Thousands of "hard core unemployables" were given job
training, many of them by U.S. Steel. . . . The open, burning city dump was safely
filled in, and the sewage system began to be cleaned up. In the context of Gary's
experience of city government, the reforms were dramatic.[17]

    The new housing construction and building code enforcement policies
were indicative of the impact the Hatcher administration had on the community. Gary's housing stock, especially its rental housing, had been
decaying for many years. Critics attributed housing decay to ineffectual
building code enforcement by the city's building inspectors and to the fact
that there had been no public housing completed in Gary for sixteen years
prior to 1968. In the previous previous forty years, there had been only 260
rental units constructed in Gary, public or private. According to Hatcher,
47 percent of the existing structures required "either major rehabilitation
or clearance."[18]
    During Hatcher's first few months in office, building inspections rose
dramatically. During one month 4184 buildings were checked for possible
violations; during the previous administration, only 331 buildings were
checked for a similar period. At the same time that existing structures were
being improved to conform to building code standards, new public housing
was being constructed at a remarkable pace. Almost monthly the Hatcher
administration announced plans for and opened new public housing. The
addition of 4500 new housing units—including the 550-unit development
sponsored by the US Steel Corporation and administered by Gary's Urban
League—provided new housing opportunities for many of Gary's ghettoized blacks and improved the appearance of many neighborhoods.
    Hatcher's next most important achievement involved manpower de-
velopment and job-training programs.

The manpower development programs touched over 10,000 Gary residents from
high school students to steel workers. The manpower programs were coordinated
with housing and physical development programs. These programs were also seen
as instruments for achieving economic diversification. Manpower trainees and their
instructors, for example, expanded and improved the Gary airport; this effort,
coupled with the projected growth of the Port of Indiana in the next few years,
promises to provide a mass infusion of new jobs into the area within the present
decade.[19]

The immediate beneficiaries of these programs tended to be Gary's blacks and Latin-Americans. This caused a great deal of unhappiness among the city's whites, who saw little personal benefit from the federal programs. However, enough money from the development programs was spent locally that the support of the business community was assured.

Another major impact of Hatcher's mayorship was the professionalization of city government. In the past, most of the city's high-paying jobs went to political allies of the mayor, with little consideration given for their qualifications. Hatcher made extensive efforts to recruit top-flight administrators for the city government. These efforts were not always successful, either because the man Hatcher had in mind would not move to Gary, or the job did not offer a competitive wage. Nevertheless, the mayor was generally successful in his departure from the patronage staffing policies of previous administrations. Hatcher even managed to recruit some well-trained black professionals for jobs in planning, law enforcement, and general administration. Three special assistants were also hired with special two-year, twenty-five-thousand-dollar salaries funded by the Ford Foundation and Gary's Committee of 100.

Another area of substantial administrative change was the reorganization of the city government's executive branch. The mayor first established a department of Program development, which was charged with the responsibility for correcting administrative defects in the government's chain-of-command and weeding out incompetent and corrupt city employees held over from previous administrations. A cabinet soon replaced the former system of thirty-two department heads reporting directly to the mayor. Under the new system the departments were organized into five general departments headed by the mayor's three special assistants (for public safety and law enforcement, housing and community development, and fiscal and personnel administration), the city attorney, and the city engineer. This new structure had the effect of focusing the mayor's attention, simplifying his span of control, and coordinating policy.

The number and percentage of blacks and Latin-Americans employed by the city and appointed to boards and commissions rose dramatically. By 1969, blacks or Latin-Americans headed fourteen of Gary's twenty-seven departments including the police, fire, general service, and planning departments, as well as manning the offices of the city controller, city attorney, and corporation council. Many of the operating units of the city government became almost all black or Latin-American, and their number and influence increased in the police and fire departments. The control of sensitive boards and commissions like the school board also changed from white to black.

There was also an increase in the number of black contractors and suppliers doing business with City Hall. Most notable was the award of a contract for the construction of a fire station and another $1 million contract for demolition work connected with Gary's Urban Renewal Program to Inter-City Contractor's Services, an amalgamation of small firms that could not bid on major contracts individually.[20] Besides awarding contracts to black businessmen, the mayor also had some success at influencing white contractors and suppliers doing business with the city to hire more black employees.

One of the most important changes in the city government occurred in the police department. When Hatcher appointed James Hilton police chief (Hilton was succeeded after two years in office by a black, Charles Boone), he gave him two goals : cut down on street crime and drive organized crime and vice out of the city.[21] It was widely rumored that organized crime thrived in Gary because it was linked to senior officers on the police force. Hatcher reorganized the police department and cracked down on organized crime, breaking the ties between organized crime and some members of the police force.

During the first two years of Hatcher's administration, the police department was increased from 276 to 350 officers, new police cars were bought and old ones were repaired, and police-community relations offices were opened. By the middle of 1969, Hatcher could show statistics that crime rates had dropped 13 percent during the first half of 1969 compared to a similar period in 1968, and the more obvious manifestations of vice like betting parlors and houses of prostitution had been driven underground.[22]

But not all of Hatcher's efforts to reform the city's police were successful. On more than one occasion, the mayor attempted to discipline some policemen or purge some senior officers from the department. These efforts failed because only one of the three members of the police civil service commission was appointed by the mayor; one of the other two members was appointed by the city council and the other was appointed by the city's police officers. While Hatcher's anticrime program met with mixed success, his good relations with the city's black youth gangs yielded some positive benefits. Aside from a two-hour spree in July 1968 in which three stores were set afire, some looting occurred, and 127 people were arrested, the city experienced no prolonged rioting and violence of the kind that swept many cities after the assassination of Dr. Martin Luther King.

Legally, Gary's mayor is not supposed to get involved in the city's school system. However, because they appointed the school board, former mayors influenced school construction, promotions, and contracts. Hatcher attempted to stay out of the school system's everyday affairs and leave these matters to the discretion of professional administrators. However, because the school system was in desperate financial condition and experienced a teachers' strike and a students' boycott, the mayor inevitably became involved with educational affairs. Despite his considerable peace-keeping activities, Hatcher's major contribution to the education system came from his ability to generate federal and foundation funds earmarked for educational services and innovative programs.

Besides his substantive impact on the city, Hatcher also had a profound and controversial symbolic impact. During his term in office, Gary's whites and blacks had divergent perceptions about the performance of city government and the quality of life in Gary.[23] Many whites chose to regard the Hatcher mayoralty as a bad experience to be endured until they could move to the suburbs. Under previous administrations, Gary's whites enjoyed open access to almost every city official and agency. After Hatcher's election, they were less visible at City Hall. In contrast, blacks from all walks of life became more welcome in the offices of city officials and agencies.

But no matter how strong Hatcher's commitment to reversing the direction of Gary's decline, or his impact, enormous unsolved city problems remained. Pollution of the air and water by US Steel mixed with the dilapidated wooden structures of most city neighborhoods combined to make Gary an ugly and depressing place to live or to visit. Crime rates remained high. Whites and blacks continued to openly detest each other. And despite all the employment programs sponsored by the federal government, many of Gary's blacks remained uneducated, unemployed, underemployed, undernourished, and poorly housed. In short, Gary faced so many problems that are deeply rooted in its history and American society that local efforts could only improve conditions at the margin of daily life.

In summary, it has been argued that in a racially polarized community like Gary, Indiana, effective mayoral leadership is possible. Because Mayor Hatcher was unwilling to co-opt his opponents through bargains he considered odious, he chose to adopt a distinctly racially partisan leadership style and used large amounts of federal funds to finance a variety of new programs aimed primarily at improving the living conditions and employment opportunities of the city's black population.

The leadership behavior of Richard Hatcher resulted in the *centralization* of politics, the *mobilization* of community resources, and substantial *innovation*. However, Hatcher's coalition did not include whites on equal terms with blacks. Instead, the mayor developed a coalition that differentially incorporated whites as minority participants and recipients of political rewards and benefits. From a pluralist perspective, Hatcher's failure to *integrate* white interest groups and institutions into a biracial coalition would be an indicator of the mayor's ineffective leadership. However, a conflict orientation would regard his ability to activate innovative programs and *exclude* these groups and institutions as a sign of effective mayoral leadership.

Notes

1. For discussions of nondecision making in Gary prior to Hatcher's election, see: Edward Greer, "The 'Liberation' of Gary, Indiana," *Trans-action* 8 (January 1971), pp. 30-39; "Limits of Black Mayoral Reform in Gary: Air Pollution and Corporate Power," a paper delivered at the 1973 Annual Meeting of the American Political Science Association, New Orleans, Louisiana, September 4-8, 1973; Matthew A. Crenson *The Un-Politics of Air Pollution: A Study of Non-Decision Making in the Cities* (Baltimore: Johns Hopkins Press, 1971); William E. Nelson, Jr., *Black Politics in Gary: Problems and Prospects* (Washington, D.C.: Joint Center for Political Studies, 1972); and Alex Poinsett, *Black Power Gary Style: The Making of Mayor Richard Gordon Hatcher* (Chicago: Johnson Publishing Co., 1970).

2. See Godfrey Hodgson and George Crile, "Gary: Epitaph for a Model City," *Washington Post,* 4 March 1973, p. B2.

3. For discussions of the dynamics of Gary's Democratic machine, see Thomas F. Thompson, *Public Administration in the Civil City of Gary, Indiana* (unpublished Ph.D. dissertation, Indiana University, 1960); Warner Bloomberg, Jr., *The Power Structure of an Industrial Community* (unpublished Ph.D. dissertation, University of Chicago, 1961); Phillips Cutright, *Party Organization and Voting Behavior* (unpublished Ph.D. dissertation, University of Chicago, 1960); and, Peter H. Rossi and Phillips Cutright, "The Impact of Party Organization in an Industrial Setting," in Morris Janowitz, ed. *Community Political Systems* (New York: The Free Press, 1961).

4. Wilson has observed:

The machine can flourish in the Negro wards largely because of the status and needs of the Negro. The incentives it can offer are still attractive to many Negroes, whereas they have largely lost their appeal to other ethnic groups which have risen farther. Low-paying jobs, political favors, and material assistance are still as important to many Negroes as they once were to foreign-born whites. The Negroes, unlike the Irish, have not priced themselves out of the market.

James Q. Wilson, *Negro Politics: The Search for Leadership* (New York: The Free Press, 1960), p. 54.

5. See Chuck Stone, *Black Political Power in America,* rev. ed. (New York: Delta Books, 1970), p. 220.

6. Ibid., p. 221.

7. Ibid., p. 223; and Jeffry K. Hadden, Louis H. Masotti, and Victor Thiessen, "The Making of the Negro Mayors 1967," *Trans-action* 5 (January-February 1968), pp. 21-30.

8. See Hadden, Masotti, and Thiessen, "The Making of the Negro Mayors 1967," p. 28.

9. See Nelson, *Black Politics in Gary,* p. 29.

10. Quoted in Poinsett, *Black Power Gary Style,* pp. 99, 102. Banfield and Wilson's description of the municipal reform movement seems to fit at least one dimension of Hatcher's administration.

From its beginnings to the present, the municipal reform movement has had the goals of eliminating corruption, increasing efficiency, and making local government in some sense more democratic. The relative emphasis that reformers have placed upon these goals has of course varied with the person, the place, and the time; but reform has always and everywhere stood for some combination of the three.

Edward C. Banfield and James Q. Wilson, *City Politics* (New York: Vintage Books, 1963), p. 138; see also Duane Lockard, *The Politics of State and Local Government* 2nd ed. (New York: Macmillan Co., 1969), pp. 386-89.

11. Interview, Gary, Indiana, July 1969.

12. See Poinsett, *Black Power Gary Style,* pp. 146-49.

13. Interview, Gary, Indiana, July 22, 1969.

14. For scathing critiques of US Steel's policies, see Greer, "Limits of Black Mayoral Reform in Gary: Air Pollution and Corporate Policy;" Paul Booth and Edward Greer, "Big Steel in the Calumet: A Tale of Two Cities," *Social Policy* 3 (July-August 1973); Crenson, *The Un-Politics of Air Pollution;* and, George Crile, "A Tax Assessor Has Many Friends," *Harper's Magazine* 245 (November 1972), pp. 102-11.

15. In many ways Hatcher has confronted the audience-constituency paradox described by Wilson. See James Q. Wilson, "The Mayors vs. the Cities," *Public Interest* 16 (Summer 1969), pp. 25-37.

16. An interesting debate concerning Gary's health as a "Model City" appeared in *Washington Post* in March 1973. See Godfrey Hodgson and George Crile, "Gary: Epitaph for a Model City," 4 March 1973, pp. B1-2; and "More on 'Gary: An Epitaph for a Model City,'" *Washington Post,* 25 March 1973, p. C7; also James O. Gibson and Geno Baroni, "Gary: Another View," *Washington Post,* 18 March 1973, p. K2.

17. Hodgson and Crile, "Gary: Epitaph For a Model City," p. B2.

18. "2000 New Homes Up: Hatcher," *Gary Post-Tribune,* 18 December 1969, p. 12.

19. Gibson and Baroni, "Gary: Another View."

20. Poinsett, *Black Power Gary Style,* p. 122.

21. Interview, Gary, Indiana, July 22, 1969.

22. See "Murder, Rape Up: Thefts Down," *Gary Post-Tribune* 26 July 1969.

23. For a discussion of white hostility to black power in Gary, see Marshall Frady, "Gary, Indiana," *Harper's Magazine* 239 (August 1969), pp. 35-45. Some survey data is reported in Sheldon Stryker, "The Urban Scene: Observations from Research," *The Review* (Bloomington, Indiana: Alumni Association of the College of Arts and Sciences Graduate School, August 1969), pp. 8-17; Thomas F. Pettigrew, *Racially Separate or Together?* (New York: McGraw-Hill Book Co., 1971), pp. 236-51; and, Howard Schuman and Barry Gruenberg, "The Impact of City on Racial Attitudes," *American Journal of Sociology* 76 (September 1970), pp. 213-61.

6 Birmingham: The Politics of Hegemony

Background and Structure

From Birmingham's founding in 1871, until George Seibels's 1967 election, the city's mayors and business leaders were simultaneously committed to maintaining two socioeconomic patterns that proved to be incompatible in the 1960s: racial segregation and economic growth. During most of this period, local decision making was dominated by the managers of Birmingham's steel industry, especially US Steel, the area's largest employer. By carefully manipulating elected officials, the steel industry was able to influence zoning, taxation, annexation, and pollution policies at the city, county, and state levels of government. The industry's interest in growth, however, stopped at economic self-interest. In the area of race relations, it adopted a posture of nonintervention in local affairs, but it did adopt some local practices by establishing separate recruitment and promotion systems for black and white employees.[1] To maintain their electoral popularity, the city's mayors (and from 1911 to 1963 its commissioners) vigorously enforced the community's rigid pattern of racial segregation and maintained as low a level of city services as the city's largely working-class population would tolerate.

Throughout its first hundred years, Birmingham's industries attracted thousands of unskilled and semiskilled laborers from surrounding areas. These workers brought with them southern attitudes about racial segregation and a fear of competition from low-cost black labor, creating what Martin Luther King described as probably "the most thoroughly segregated city in the United States."[2] Since black voters comprised only a tiny fraction of Birmingham's electorate until 1965 and black protests were met with repression, political leadership in Birmingham was oriented toward maintaining the status quo through racial hegemony and fiscal austerity.

During the Depression, Birmingham experienced massive unemployment and economic stagnation. The city's economy recovered during World War II and the Korean War, but after 1953, the steel mills stopped expanding and began to automate. Unemployment soared, and northern firms, becoming more conscious of civil rights, were reluctant to support southern patterns of racial segregation by investing in the city.

Throughout the fifties, Birmingham's commissioners refused to raise taxes for public works improvements and social services or accede to black

85

demands to end segregation. By 1960 unemployment was extensive, the downtown business district was stagnant, and the city's middle class, appalled by the physical and economic condition of the city and the repressive racism of the commissioners and police department, fled to the suburbs, some leaving the Birmingham area entirely.

Against this background, a group of attorneys, businessmen, and labor leaders began a quiet movement in 1961 to oust the city's three conservative commissioners by reorganizing Birmingham's government. Their primary target was the commissioner of public safety, Theophilus Eugene "Bull" Connor, who, with the exception of four years during the mid-fifties, had held office since 1937. Under Connor, Birmingham's police force had become the major weapon of racists bent on suppressing black efforts to ease segregation. Because Birmingham's commissioners were virtually autonomous in the functional areas they supervised (the president of the commission bore the official title of mayor, but in law and in practice did not interfere in the other commissioners' domains) and because Connor was the most successful political campaigner active in Birmingham politics, to change police practices meant replacing Connor; and removing Connor required a change in the whole structure of city government.

The reform movement gained momentum after a group of "freedom riders" were badly beaten by a white mob while the city's police were ordered to enjoy the Mother's Day holiday with their families at home.[3] More downtown businessmen joined in the low-profile campaign against Connor after he used building code enforcement as a weapon to prevent the upgrading of black employees and the limited desegregation of some facilities in retail outlets, conditions that the businessmen had agreed to as part of a settlement with local black leaders. Finally, the movement gained even more momentum after the commissioners repealed the budget of the park and recreation board, forcing the parks to close in response to a desegregation order from the US Supreme Court.

The severity of these measures aroused fears among businessmen that the city's already weak economy might be damaged by any further erosion of its image. After an extensive study by a committee of the Birmingham Bar Association, a broadly representative committee of five hundred citizens was formed to first petition and then campaign for a reorganization plan. While Connor's conduct was clearly a major issue, the reorganization proponents publicly avoided any mention of Connor or racial issues. Instead, they stressed the potential improvements in economy, efficiency, and accountability to be gained by "modernizing" Birmingham's government around a single executive and a nine-member city council.

In the referendum held late in 1962, the mayor-council alternative won by a clear majority over the commission form and a poorly supported council-manager proposal. The commissioners challenged the referendum in the courts, arguing that they were legally entitled to serve their four-year terms, which would not expire until 1965. While the courts were left to decide the legality of the referendum, the initiative specified that an election of a mayor and a nine-member city council would be held in March 1963.

The new form of city government limited the formal authority of Birmingham's mayor. Under Alabama law, the state legislature retained many powers over local affairs and decentralized responsibility for a great deal of local policy-making to a variety of semiautonomous boards and commissions. Since the proponents of the reorganization sought to check many of the excesses of the commissioners, a weakened executive corresponded neatly with their objectives. However, when the reformers first began to explore reorganization, they discovered the only option available to Birmingham under state law was a mayor-council plan that basically was a slightly modified version of a council-manager arrangement. To strengthen the state's mayor-council option, the mayor of Birmingham was given some additional powers: an executive veto that could be overruled by a two-thirds vote of the city council, an administrative assistant, and a salary of $24,000 rather than the $12,000 prescribed by the original state statute.[4] Despite the fact that Birmingham is the only city in Alabama to operate under a system of local government that resembles a strong mayor form, local government is best understood as a council-manager form with an elected mayor instead of an appointed manager being granted an executive veto.

Birmingham's mayor is primarily constrained by his appointment powers. While he can appoint department heads from a list of three nominees submitted by the autonomous Jefferson County personnel board, he cannot remove department heads or other employees protected by the civil-service system and can only discipline city employees after demonstrating "sufficient cause." The mayor's influence over Birmingham's boards and commissions is also limited because the city council has sole authority to appoint the members of the city's most important boards.[5] The mayor is left with appointment powers that encompass a few relatively unimportant boards like the fifty-one member beautification board. Once appointed, the members of such important boards as the board of education and the park and recreation board serve long and staggered terms and are given a great deal of authority to make policy and spend city revenue. The mayor's appointment powers are so limited that until 1973 even appointees to his immediate staff had to be tested and screened by the personnel board.

The mayor's influence is also constrained by Birmingham's electoral system. The city's elections are nonpartisan, and the city council is elected at-large. Five councilmen stand for reelection every two years, with the four receiving the most votes elected for four-year terms while the fifth-highest serves a two-year term. Because local tradition discourages slate making, candidates for the council usually run independently, thereby limiting the mayor's control over the composition of the city council.

The division of responsibility between Birmingham city government and other governmental entities also complicates the task of mayoral leadership. The county government retains responsibility for such essential services as health code enforcement, and its sheriff's department and public works activities often have an impact upon the city. Also, the more than thirty suburban municipalities in Jefferson County replicate many of Birmingham's services, and their reluctance to merge or integrate their services with city departments has often produced strains between the city and the suburban governments. Finally, the rural-dominated state government, particularly since the election of George Wallace as governor, has tended to adopt an indifferent posture toward Birmingham's problems, retarding the city's highway construction program and its plans to annex surrounding suburbs.

The formal powers granted Birmingham's mayor provided him the visibility to represent city government, but not the resources to centralize policy making and control implementation. At various times proposals have been made to strengthen the mayoralty by limiting the autonomy of boards and commissions, allowing partisan elections, and creating authority for the mayor to freely remove and appoint department heads. But despite continual problems of mayoral authority, proposals to strengthen the mayoralty have been frustrated by the resistance of the state legislature and the city council.

In addition to these legal parameters, the influence of Birmingham's mayor has been limited by the city's economic and ecological condition. For years, the city's commissioners refused to raise taxes for public works projects or improve salaries for city employees. Throughout the twentieth century, Birmingham consistently remained near the bottom of rankings of municipal governments on per capita expenditures for public services. By refusing to improve or maintain the city's physical facilities, the commissioners "mortgaged the future" by allowing an agenda of public works projects to accumulate that absorbed nearly all the slack resources generated during the decade following the reorganization of the city government.[6]

Finally, Birmingham's mayors are constrained by racial polarization and the city's history of violent and repressive racial conflict. Even before the 1963 election, it was obvious that Birmingham's blacks were becoming more politically powerful and future mayors would have to confront persistent black demands for representation in policy making, equality of service distribution, and affirmative action in governmental hiring practices. But because Birmingham's electorate remained at least two-thirds white throughout the 1960s and many whites remained opposed to racial accommodation in any form, accommodating black demands and forging racial peace required mayors with a keen sense of compromise politics and willingness to absorb stinging criticism from both sides.

The extent of racial polarization in Birmingham was vividly brought to national attention during 1963, when Martin Luther King led demonstrations aimed at ending the city's most offensive segregation practices. The city government was in a particularly poor position to act to minimize the effects of what became six weeks of demonstrations, police brutality, and retaliatory bombings of black homes, businesses, and churches, because during the height of the chaos—from April 15 to May 23, 1963—it had two governments and two mayors. The referendum to change the form of city government was still being contested in the courts when Albert Boutwell defeated ''Bull'' Connor for the mayorship in March 1963. Since the referendum specified that the new mayor and city council should take office April 15, and the commissioners refused to vacate City Hall until the court case was settled, the locus of legal authority to govern the city was in doubt. King, having delayed his campaign until after the election at the request of local black leaders, who feared demonstrations might lead to a white backlash that would elect Connor, began the demonstrations shortly after Boutwell's inauguration. Connor responded by using police dogs and firehoses against King's demonstrators, creating a scene of repression that captured national attention. Connor's brutal response and a series of unsolved bombings culminating in the deaths of four black girls attending Sunday school were the last acts of overt repressive segregation that the city experienced. A few weeks afterwards, the Alabama Supreme Court ruled that the Boutwell administration was the rightful government of the city.

Despite initial optimism that the new government would depolarize the city, too many deeply held attitudes about race persisted to allow any major changes in race relations. As Holloway observed in the late sixties:

All in all, Birmingham is a peculiar combination of traditional racial attitudes and an urban setting. Elements that contribute to this pattern include the city's manufacturing background, the type of men attracted to work in mine and factory, the absentee ownership, the stagnation brought by the Depression, and the recent influx of poor, intolerant migrants. The influence of state politics has been another potent element. The result has been a city that has long retained an obsession with race and has lacked the expansive, forward-looking outlook and leadership of an Atlanta. A politics of race rather than a politics of economics has been the rule.[7]

Electoral Politics

Birmingham's electoral campaigns have always—either overtly or covertly—involved ''the race issue.'' Since the mid-fifties, however, there has been a shift toward greater emphasis on public works projects, taxation, governmental efficiency, and the protection of single-family residential neighborhoods from urban renewal, highway construction, and apartment house developments. Nevertheless, candidates for public office continue to be evaluated by most voters on the basis of how much attention they appear to be willing to devote to demands for change from the black community.

Because Birmingham's elections are nonpartisan and the Republican and Democratic parties maintain a low profile in local elections, electoral campaigns have been conducted by ad hoc organizations assembled by the candidates themselves. Except for the election of 1963, Birmingham's voters have never turned out in large numbers to vote in municipal elections. Since 1965 the city's electorate has tended to split into three voting blocs of approximately equal size: working-class white segregationists, middle-class white moderates, and blacks. The blocs tend to support favorite candidates in general elections and cluster into two-bloc coalitions in runoff elections. If two blocs support the same mayoral candidate or council candidates, there is usually a large winning margin, as in Boutwell's 1963 election, Seibels's 1971 reelection, and the 1973 city council race. When a bloc fragments, as the black vote did in 1967, victory margins tend to be much slimmer.

Because Birmingham's electoral politics are ad hoc, the *Birmingham News*, the larger and more influential of the city's two white-owned daily newspapers, has played an important role in local elections. A member of the Newhouse chain, the *News* has taken a conservative, business-oriented stance on most major issues and has endorsed a succession of successful council and mayoral candidates. Through the leadership of S. Vincent Townsend, officially assistant to the publisher of the *News* but unofficially the most powerful political figure in the city, the newspaper has exerted such an important influence on local politics that its endorsement is the single most important resource for council and mayoral candidates.[8]

In November 1962, after fifty-two years, the commission form of government was voted out of power. Four candidates declared their intention to seek the mayoralty in the election scheduled for early in 1963, and over seventy candidates filed petitions for the nine seats on the new city council. The incumbent mayor and president of the commission, Arthur J. Haines, decided against seeking reelection under the new arrangement, but the two other commissioners, J.D. Waggoner and "Bull" Connor, decided to run. They were joined by Tom King, who had been defeated by Haines in 1961, and Albert Boutwell, a former state legislator and lieutenant governor.

Boutwell (17,437), Connor (13,788), and King (11,639) led the voting in the general election, with Waggoner finishing far behind (1872). Since none of the candidates was able to muster a majority, a runoff election between Boutwell and Connor was scheduled for the following month.

The Boutwell-Connor contest was a choice between styles rather than ideologies. Both men were firmly established as segregationists, but Boutwell's credentials as a diplomat stood in marked contrast to Connor's reputation as a hard-line segregationist. Boutwell's campaign stressed that Birmingham's future was at stake and the city was being controlled by political leaders who discouraged economic growth, an appeal that attracted white moderates and black voters.[9] Over 75 percent of Birmingham's registered voters turned out to vote in the runoff, a record for municipal elections, with blacks joining white moderates to help Boutwell decisively defeat Connor (29,636 to 21,648).

At his inauguration Boutwell pledged to attack the city's unemployment, end deficit spending, reopen the parks, launch a broader program of public works projects, and reconcile racial differences.[10] Shortly afterwards, the new city council moved to restore racial peace by repealing every one of the city's segregation ordinances. Boutwell followed that by helping to reopen the city's parks and pushing forward highway construction and urban renewal projects. In 1964 the new government received a vote of confidence when voters overwhelmingly rejected a proposal to return to the commission form and also approved a 1 percent sales tax that provided a major infusion of new funds for the city government. In August 1965 voters approved a large bond issue calling for the expenditure of $14 million for street resurfacing, sewers, and the coverage of open storm drains.

But despite the changes, Boutwell was attacked for his failure to provide the city with "positive, dynamic, aggressive leadership."[11] Critics charged that the city government was sluggish in implementing urban renewal, highway construction, police reform, school construction, street improvement, air pollution control, and equal employment opportunity programs. As the 1967 election approached, Boutwell's popularity waned. Segregationists accused Boutwell of pushing integration too far, while white moderates and blacks were impatient with the rate of change as swimming pools remained closed and public housing projects continued to be segregated.

Boutwell faced four energetic challengers in the 1967 mayoral campaign: George G. Seibels, Jr., a city councilman; George Young, an attorney and a political newcomer; Richard Dill, a state representative; and Earl Langner, a former recorders court judge. To nearly everyone's surprise, Boutwell finished third in the general election and was eliminated from the runoff. In the runoff, Seibels (27,709) defeated Young (25,338) by gaining strong support from middle- and upper-income white voters, while Young won slight majorities of the black and lower-income white vote.

George Seibels was a departure from previous Birmingham mayors. He was neither a Democrat, professional politician, or a segregationist. Furthermore, Seibels was dynamic and outgoing, a contrast to the styles of Haines and Boutwell. As a city councilman, Seibels had shown more interest than other councilmen in improving governmental operations; and as chairman of the council's committee on public safety, he promoted increased police professionalism and the hiring of more black police officers.[12]

During his first term, Seibels enjoyed great popularity throughout Birmingham. The city's economy, social climate, and national image continued to improve. New industries opened in Birmingham, unemployment declined, and several new downtown office buildings and major highway projects were completed.[13] Despite some attempts to minimize his contributions to Birmingham's economic, physical, and spiritual rejuvenation, Seibels's activist style persuaded enough people that he was at least partially responsible for the changes that his reelection seemed assured.

In 1971, George Young was again Seibels's major challenger. Young charged the mayor with failure to adequately modernize city services and with squandering city revenue. Young called for the repeal of the 1 percent occupational tax that Seibels had sponsored and charged that the city had spent millions of dollars on projects that were "ill-conceived, ill-planned, ill-advised and most of all mismanaged."[14]

Seibels met Young's charges by campaigning with unusual zeal for an incumbent. He won the enthusiastic endorsement of the *Birmingham News* and most of the city's major political organizations, including the Jefferson County Progressive Democratic Council, Birmingham's major black political organization. Seibels (37,124) easily defeated Young (21,482) and three other candidates (3511), and because he captured 59.8 percent of the total vote, he was reelected without a runoff.

The large margin of Seibels's victory can be traced directly to his lopsided winning margins in black precincts. Overall, the mayor received an estimated 85 to 90 percent of the black vote and carried some black precincts with almost 99 percent of the vote. In contrast, Young, who aimed his campaign at white working-class disenchantment with changes in the city, barely carried white blue-collar precincts.

Seibels's impressive victory should have greatly strengthened his leadership position in the city, but the 1971 election also changed the composition of the city council. In 1971 voters elected three new councilmen who were extremely progressive in their attitudes toward improving the city and encouraging black economic development. Almost immediately the council split into progressive and conservative voting blocs. The progressives—the three new members plus a long-term incumbent—pressed for better long-range planning, greater neighborhood participation in policy making, and the appointment of more blacks and women to the city's bureaucracy and its boards and commissions. On a number of issues they were joined by the first black to be elected to the city council, Arthur Shores, a noted civil-rights attorney and a political moderate, who was first appointed to the council in 1968 and was then elected to a full four-year term in 1969. Since the progressive bloc could only muster five votes, it controlled a bare majority, but not the two-thirds majority needed to override mayoral vetoes.

The development of the progressive bloc set the stage for the highly contested 1973 city council election. After the general election, two incumbent councilwomen were reelected, leaving six candidates competing for the three remaining seats in the runoff. Although each of the six candidates initially ran independently, they were soon clustered into two slates composed of three incumbents—two white conservatives and Shores—and three challengers, who were young black professionals.[15] Critics of the three incumbents characterized them as "middle-aged men who identified with most middle-class aspirations for the city . . . notable for their cautious approaches to social problems and for their willingness to go along with programs which often required heavy expenditures for projects which are largely civic cosmetics."[16] In contrast, most political observers assumed that if the challengers were to win the runoff, the city council would change from a moderate to a far more liberal orientation.

Fearing a radical change in the city council's policy-making posture and white reaction to the militancy of the three black challengers, the officers of Birmingham's most important business group, Operation New Birmingham (ONB), organized a fund-raising drive to support the incumbents through an ad hoc committee, the Birmingham Action Group (BAG). BAG raised over $18,000 in a few days and launched an implicitly racist media and phone campaign to get out the white vote for the incumbents.[17]

BAG's campaign succeeded. The white vote in the runoff nearly doubled as the incumbents defeated the challengers by a two-to-one margin. Responding to angry critics, BAG's officers denied they were directly affiliated with ONB or that their campaign was intended to arouse racism among Birmingham's whites. But the disclosure of BAG's list of contributors revealed a substantial overlap with the more active members of ONB, and an analysis of its advertising revealed that BAG had indeed used racism to get out the white vote.[18]

While BAG's campaign was a short-run victory for the business community and white conservatives, its potential long-run implications were more profound. For the first time the pervasive involvement of the business community in manipulating local elections and policy making came clearly before the public view.[19] Reaction to BAG's tactics from both blacks and whites gave a clear signal to Birmingham's business leaders that they could no longer expect to speak for the well-being of the whole city if they also intended to participate in local politics as partisans.

Policy Politics and Leadership Structure

As early as 1964, it had become obvious to political observers that the revised city charter failed to provide Birmingham with a powerful mayor, and that the conservative, soft-spoken Boutwell would not take the initiative to substantially reverse the city's economic, ecological, and social disintegration. To initiate change, extra governmental activity was needed. In the first few months following the racial disturbances, some of the city's business leaders formed Operation New Birmingham (ONB) to improve the city's national image, to increase industrial development, to revitalize the downtown business district, to serve as a mediating influence between the black and white communities, and most of all, to spur local governmental activity to foster these goals.[20] Over the decade from 1964 to 1974, there emerged a pattern of ONB influence so pervasive that at times the organization's leadership supplanted the centrality of the mayor and city council in the formulation of public policy and in the selection of appointees to important boards and commissions.

ONB's involvement in local politics was legitimized by the biracial composition of its membership and the active involvement of Birmingham's leading black businessman, A.G. Gaston, president of the Booker T. Washington Insurance Company. However, critics charged that the biracial nature of ONB was deceptive, because Gaston and his associates, including Arthur Shores, represented business rather than black interests on ONB committees and were indifferent to the needs of the city's black poor.

The symbolic changes in Birmingham's leadership structure had its greatest impact on the level of political activism within the black community. Between 1963 and 1969, the quiescence of the black community produced few new demands for greater economic opportunity or improved services. The complacency of the black community was attributable to the widely shared view that the major battle for civil rights had been fought in 1963 and that changes in federal laws, local government, and business involvement were alleviating the city's most repressive segregation practices.

In 1969, however, a series of police brutality incidents led Gaston and other black influentials to sign a protest letter warning that they could not prevent acts of civil disobedience by black youths if police practices were not changed. The militant tone of the letter shocked Birmingham's white leadership and led to the formation of the Community Affairs Committee (CAC) to mediate race relations. CAC was originally composed of twenty-seven members: nine from the city government, including the mayor, police chief, and the superintendent of schools; nine white businessmen; and nine black professionals and businessmen. In 1969, CAC had black and white co-chairmen: Lucius Pitts, president of Miles College, and Cecil Bauer, president of the South Central Bell Telephone Company.

CAC was similar in composition to an ad hoc committee that had proved successful in reaching the compromise that ended the 1963 turmoil. As an affiliate of ONB, CAC's specific purpose was to provide a forum for interracial dialogue and an arena for bargaining. CAC attempted to improve the city's race relations by building a dialogue between black and white elites, prodding city officials to improve city services to black neighborhoods, persuading local businessmen to provide more employment opportunities for Birmingham's blacks, and promoting the accommodation of more blacks into elective and appointive policy-making positions.[21] In particular, CAC tackled a variety of specific problems that concerned blacks, like food stamp distribution, proposed public works projects, and the hiring of more black city employees.

While CAC was successful in influencing local policy making and easing racial tensions, many younger political activists, black and white, regarded CAC as an unrepresentative gerontocracy composed of elites who were more concerned with preserving racial peace than social progress.[22] In addition, many black activists criticized CAC's black members for being subservient to the committee's white leadership because they had been selected by the white majority of CAC membership and tended to maintain conservative bargaining styles. To ease criticism, CAC's membership was gradually expanded, and early in 1974 a proposal was being seriously considered to add younger black and white civic leaders by expanding the group to over sixty members.[23]

The composition of ONB and CAC's membership helps to explain the behavior of Birmingham's elite and the city's policy politics. Aside from Gaston, a few large downtown merchants, and some major real estate developers, Birmingham's business community was represented by the managers of absentee-owned corporations who lived in Birmingham's suburbs and were not even voters in the city.[24] This pattern of membership influenced ONB/CAC roles as agenda-setters for city politics. Under the leadership of S. Vincent Townsend, chairman of the board of ONB, the organizations promoted business interests while buffering neighborhood demands and guiding racial accommodation. Through adroit public relations, ONB and CAC convinced citizens that they performed a valuable service by promoting citywide progress; both organizations were granted a great degree of latitude and legitimacy by the community. The relationship between ONB/CAC and city politics was further obscured (aside from the BAG incident in the 1973 city council campaign) by ONB's quasi-governmental contract activities on behalf of the city government for public relations and lobbying.[25] ONB was the only private group in the city to have an office in City Hall. The fact that the membership of ONB and CAC was biracial blurred the consensual nature of Birmingham's power structure, which dominated the local political agenda, made policy, and assured its implementation.

Mayor Seibels's leadership style and approach to Birmingham's problems neatly complemented the elite domination and manipulation of local politics. While the mayor was widely regarded as "hardworking, sincere, dedicated, enthusiastic, dignified, and polished,"[26] critics observed that:

1. The Mayor was handicapped by his lack of experience in managing large-scale organizations and multimillion dollar budgets.

2. His approach to politics tended to be based on boosterism and the naive view that changes could be made without confrontation or bargaining, even when entrenched interests were adversely affected.

3. He tried to do too much himself and failed to build a first-rate staff which could augment his administrative and political weaknesses.

4. Because he abhorred conflict and criticism, he avoided being forceful when dealing with city department heads and state, county, and local officials.

5. He led such a frantic pace attending meetings, cutting ribbons, and giving speeches that he wasn't able to focus on specific problems or conduct systematic evaluations of the implementation of his policies by city departments.

6. He overestimated his popularity with the city's blacks, who grew impatient with symbolic change and began to demand more substantive changes.

7. He tended to value image-enhancing public works projects over social development and welfare projects.

8. He often failed to consult with the city council before proposing major programs that the council would have to approve and the departments would have to eventually implement.[27]

Despite these weaknesses, from 1967 to 1973, Seibels's civic activism, accessibility, and management of the city's day-to-day ceremonial affairs gave most Birmingham's citizens the impression that the mayor was running an active and progressive city government. However, when more careful observers began to differentiate the mayor's substantive achievements from his symbolic activities and convey their observations to the general public, his image as a great innovator began to erode. By late 1973, critics charged that Seibels had failed to develop long-range plans and programs for change that would have had more than a superficial or cosmetic impact on the city. Further, because he had abdicated important policy-making power to the business community by encouraging ONB and CAC political activity rather than centralizing policy making in the mayoralty, they charged that Seibels had allowed the mayorship to become a secondary institution in local politics, thereby hindering the ability of citizens to seek governmental accountability through "normal" political channels.

Some of Seibels's inability to centralize decision making can be traced to the tenure protection granted the city government's department heads by the county's civil-service system. The autonomy of Birmingham's department heads was most annoying to the mayor in his relationship with police chief Jamie Moore, an ally of "Bull" Connor. In 1967 one of Seibels's campaign pledges was to replace Moore and professionalize the city's police force. But Seibels could not force Moore to resign or fire him. Furthermore, Moore resisted any suggestion from the mayor that the police department should change its practices or hire more blacks. Although Seibels harassed Moore and even suspended him for a few days in 1969, the chief would not resign. Finally, in 1972, ONB's leaders recognized the extent to which Moore was a liability to their campaign to boost Birmingham's image and helped to get the chief appointed as an assistant to Alabama's attorney general.[28] Moore resigned to accept the new post, but it was five years after Seibels had vowed to replace him, and his removal was only accomplished after the business community decided to act.

The quiescence of the black community contributed to Seibels's image as a successful leader. Part of the explanation lies in the changes in Birmingham over the past decade and the accessibility of Seibels to the city's blacks. Seibels, for example, was the first mayor in the city's history to attend black social functions. Another reason was the legitimizing effects of black representation in political affairs, such as Gaston's involvement with ONB and CAC, the presence of Shores and Arrington on the city council and Chris McNair in the state legislature, and the appointment of numerous blacks to local boards and commissions. Finally, the black community was beset by political fragmentation; there was no single black political organization capable of sustaining a coordinated campaign to pressure for change or undertake a massive voter registration and education campaign.[29]

Birmingham's leadership structure and policy politics from 1963 to 1967 can be characterized as centralized and hegemonic; that is, even though part of the local policy-making agenda included the gradual accommodation of blacks into policy-making positions, ONB and CAC dominated the pace and nature of the change. This pattern relegated Birmingham's mayor to the role of a secondary policy-maker. Seibels, who found being part of the city's big-business community quite appealing and the present rate of racial accommodation politically comfortable, adjusted to the role with unusual enthusiasm because he basically supported the civic goals of the business elite.[30] In turn, the business community supported Seibels because his public relations skills were valuable to their campaign to upgrade the city's image. Further, the mayor's relationships with the black community added legitimacy to ONB/CAC's efforts to guide change and promote economic growth. Finally, the businessmen knew that even if Seibels objected to one of their programs, his limited formal powers, administrative skills, and political savvy would constrain his ability to upset their agenda.

Through Birmingham's structure of weak mayoral leadership and business-dominated policy making, black-white relations were mediated, economic development was spurred, and Birmingham's national reputation was improved. Meanwhile, governmental activity reflected the "bricks and mortar" orientation of the business community, while many social service needs like education, job training, public housing, and neighborhood development remained neglected.[31]

Achievements and Failures

Given George Seibels's limited formal powers and peripatetic leadership style, it is difficult to trace many of Birmingham's changes directly to the mayor's programatic initiatives. Nevertheless, throughout his term as mayor, Birmingham changed and prospered, and at the very least, Seibels can be credited with helping to create a climate in the city that facilitated economic, physical, and social development. Even though some critics charged that the mayor was much more interested in creating an image of social and physical progress than in effecting meaningful improvements in the social and ecological fabric of the city, Seibels was responsible for expanding the scope, size, and equity of public works projects and city government services; modernizing and integrating the police force; improving relations between the city government and the black community; and enhancing the city's national reputation.[32] Changes in each of these areas were accomplished by overcoming resistance from entrenched interests, and Seibels demonstrated political adroitness in facilitating them.

Seibels's most important long-range achievements were in the area of public works projects. Early in his first term, the mayor successfully campaigned for a $50 million bond issue to eliminate Birmingham's most annoying drainage ditch problems, build miniparks, improve street surfaces, install street lighting, and to help finance the "Birmingham Green," an ambitious attempt to beautify the city's main street.[33] While $26 million of the bonds were still unsold as of 1974, the expenditure of the remaining $24 million eliminated a number of problems that had persisted for decades.

Seibels also successfully campaigned for an employment tax to draw revenue from suburbanites who worked in Birmingham but who did not pay the city's property tax. The new tax, combined with a 1 percent sales tax passed during the Boutwell administration, greatly expanded the city's revenues and provided slack resources for more public works projects, higher salaries for city employees, and better governmental services and equipment.[34]

Seibels's commitment to professionalize and integrate Birmingham's police force began during his term as a city councilman. In 1972 progress toward police reform began in earnest when Thomas Parsons replaced Moore as police chief. Under Parsons, the police department was reorganized and new units, record keeping, and control systems were installed to assure police accountability. Police training was also improved, and a vigorous recruitment program was begun to attract college graduates to the force.

The number of black police officers also increased. By early 1974 there were almost forty uniformed black officers, an increase of over thirty in eighteen months.[35] After Moore's resignation, Birmingham's police force showed appreciably more professional conduct, and although much of the credit for the rapid turnabout must go to Parsons and his allies on the force, Seibels deserves recognition for choosing Parsons, keeping the pressure on Moore, and setting the direction for change.

During Seibels's first six years in office, relations between the city government and the black community improved substantially over what they had been during the Boutwell administration. By 1967 the city's public accommodations were desegregated, employment opportunities for blacks had expanded, and black political power had increased through enlarged voter registration and the appointment and election of a number of blacks to policy-making positions. When some blacks attempted to mobilize the black community to pressure for more city services, they met with resistance from black homeowners, who tended to be more impressed with the physical improvements to their neighborhoods that had been made since Seibels's election than in appeals for collective action based on racial pride.

Black reluctance to engage in the politics of racial pride can be traced to the equalization of city services to black and white neighborhoods. In the mayor's campaign to correct the worst physical problems in Birmingham, ·the city's largest open ditches and storm sewers were covered up, streets were resurfaced, and street lighting was improved. In some neighborhoods these changes were the first physical improvements that had ever been made by the city government. Also, the appointment of Arthur Shores to the chairmanship of the city council's public works committee communicated to the black community that the equalization of services was likely to continue.

The equalization of services was particularly pronounced in law enforcement. Under Parsons, police protection to the black community improved and harassment of black suspects declined. Also, garbage collection, which at one time was provided to white neighborhoods with a carry-out service, was equalized by ending the carry-out service in all neighborhoods.

Seibels also engaged in a number of other highly visible activities that built his support in the black community. For example, until Seibels's administration blacks were never allowed to drive garbage trucks and were instead assigned to handle the garbage. Under Seibels, blacks were promoted to drive garbage trucks despite angry objections by white drivers. Policy changes like these had a substantial impact on increasing Seibels's popularity in the black community and allowed the mayor to help establish the gradual pace of racial accommodation that characterized Birmingham's politics from 1967 to 1973.

Improved race relations led to Birmingham's selection in 1971 as an All America City by *Look* magazine and the National Municipal League.[36] The award reflected the city's aggressive public relations campaign and Seibels's energetic boosterism. The committee that promoted the All America City award was biracial and was composed primarily of members of the Chamber of Commerce, indicative of the business community's interest in improving the city's national image. The publicity surrounding the All America City award was similar to a number of other newspaper and magazine stories published during Seibels's first six years in office that were designed to bring favorable national attention to the city and to attract new industries and professionals to fill jobs in its expanding white-collar and medical industries.[37]

Between 1967 and 1973 a number of Birmingham's most glaring social and physical problems were corrected, but many of its most fundamental deficiencies remained. As of early 1974, for example, the city's senior high schools were not accredited; the area's suburban municipalities remained independent; few blacks were employed in better-paying city government jobs; little new public housing was under construction and virtually no "turn key" projects were being considered by the conservative housing commission; and, despite the city's impressive expenditures for urban renewal, public works and highway projects, many neighborhoods, especially those occupied by poor homeowners, continued to have poorly paved streets, open storm ditches, and inadequate street lighting. Many of Birmingham's problems were traceable to a variety of historical and structural parameters beyond any mayor's control, but a number of deficiencies are a direct result of Seibels's leadership failures, such as his inability to: (1) recognize how elite domination of city politics and the manipulative nature of the gradual accommodation of blacks into local politics might some day create grass-roots political activism in the black community; (2) build and maintain links with important policy-makers at the state and county level; (3) strengthen his staff to better control the delivery of city services; and (4) differentiate between symbolic and substantive change.

The first indication that Seibels's relations with the black community were strained occurred in 1971, when a black group blocked Birmingham's application for a $3 million Model Cities grant. The black group charged that the people who planned the proposal were not representative of the people who lived in the impacted neighborhoods. Even though the mayor was upset when Birmingham failed to receive the Model Cities grant, he refused to respond to the cause of the black group's protest by taking steps to change the composition of other boards or to include neighborhood groups in planning for the expenditure of revenue sharing money the following year.[38] The clear message for increased citizen participation expressed in the Model Cities protest was never converted into mayoral action.

The strain between the mayor and the black community caused by the Model Cities conflict reached the boiling point in late 1973, after Seibels vetoed an affirmative action bill that had been unanimously passed by the city council. After the council failed to muster the two-thirds majority needed to override the veto, a weaker bill was passed that was described by black activists as "meaningless."[39] Despite Seibels's explanation that he vetoed the original affirmative action bill because it was in conflict with state law and restricted mayoral discretion, many blacks felt betrayed and some black leaders began to accumulate evidence to prove that the city government was discriminating against blacks in its employment and promotion practices.[40]

Investigations into the racial composition of the city bureaucracy revealed that few blacks were employed in supervisory positions and that there were no black employees in some well-paid occupational categories.[41] More significantly, proponents of the stronger affirmative action bill documented cases of highly qualified black professionals who were refused employment by city agencies. By early 1974, the failure of Mayor Seibels to assure the employment of more blacks by the city government prompted a number of black politicians to begin planning for a campaign against Seibels's reelection in 1975.

Between 1963 and 1967, Birmingham's politics appeared to resemble a consociational democracy, because its elite was biracial, but the weak vertical ties between the elites, who supposedly represented the black and white communities, and the general citizenry suggest another interpretation. Because the white elite controlled the recruitment of ONB and CAC membership, they effectively controlled citizen input, making these councils less representative than if delegates had been elected or nominated by grass-roots organizations. Even the city council, elected on an at-large basis, rarely reflected with accuracy some of the intense feelings about city government held by residents of the city's neighborhoods. Finally, the composition of the city's boards and commissions was remarkably unrepresentative; many board members were arch conservatives, and some were suburbanites who did not even reside in the city.

Mayor Seibels seemed to be comfortable with this situation, even though in this structure of power, he was a secondary partner in the dominant coalition. Because Seibels was the focus of media attention, a role he seemed to relish, and the city was undergoing substantial change, the mayor appeared satisfied with his leadership role and confident that the city's best interests were being served by dividing policy and ceremonial responsibility between the economic elite and the mayor. Unfortunately, by focusing his attention on ceremonial activities, Seibels was too busy to pursue programs aimed at charting new directions or implementing innovations in local services. In short, Birmingham's power elite spurred the growth of public sector activities and encouraged some accommodation of black interests, but it did not facilitate fundamental changes in the distribution of governmental services.

Seibels also failed to establish good working relationships with officials at the state and county levels. Because he abhorred the bargaining that was characteristic of Jefferson County and Alabama state politics, communication between Birmingham city government and state, suburban, and the county governments was disjointed and unsystematic. Since the state legislature continued to set policy on taxation, government employee salaries, pension benefits, and annexation procedures, Birmingham was deprived of critical ties to the state government that might have been crucial to the long-term viability of the city government.

A number of the mayor's weaknesses can be traced to his immediate staff, which did not provide him with the capacity to control and direct the activities of the city government's administrative departments. When Judson Hodges, a city employee with forty-five years of experience, left the administration to become executive director of the State Fair Authority, the mayor was deprived of a chief administrative assistant who was intimately acquainted with the workings of the city government. Hodges's replacement and other members of the mayor's staff did not have the administrative and political experience necessary to overcome the recalcitrance of department heads and their subordinates. The weaknesses of his staff combined with Seibels's reluctance to make enemies to allow city employees to make only token efforts to carry out many of the mayor's administrative directives. Under Seibels, Birmingham's bureaucracy was reasonably free of mayoral influence and, aside from the police department, continued to be committed to protecting its autonomy and maintaining the status quo.

Finally, Seibels appears to have believed his own rhetoric about the scope and magnitude of changes in Birmingham. By overemphasizing the city's improvements and downplaying or ignoring its problems, the mayor may have become overconfident about the city's progress and his popularity among the city's voters. Seibels's inability to differentiate between short-run symbolic changes and long-run substantive improvements may have made him vulnerable to electoral defeat in 1975.

In summary, Birmingham has made enormous strides toward overcoming its negative national image and diversifying its economy. Between 1963 and 1973, the more offensive forms of racial discrimination disappeared, but the cleavage between the city's black and white population remained. Because racial conflict had to be carefully managed to avoid repetitions of the city's violent 1963 disturbances, the local business elite developed a biracial integrating mechanism to control the accommodation of blacks into Birmingham's political system. Therefore, while the form of white domination of Birmingham's politics changed and blacks made some progress toward political and economic equality, the hegemonic nature of the city's political system survived.

Birmingham's mayor since 1967, George Seibels, thrived in this pattern of political affairs. Relieved of the responsibility of tightly managing city affairs, Seibels was able to concentrate on the city's public relations, a role he appears to have enjoyed immensely. Throughout his first six years in office Birmingham remained a white hegemony and George Seibels contributed to its maintenance by successfully communicating a different image of the city. While mayoral leadership in Birmingham between 1967 and 1973 did not resemble an executive-centered coalition, it did involve some *mobilization* and *innovation* and a substantial change in the city's image.

Seibels's failure to *centralize* and *integrate* local politics around the mayoralty would be treated in pluralist analysis as signs of leadership weakness. But a conflict orientation would regard the mayor's performance as much more effective. From a conflict perspective, Seibels's contribution to the maintenance of a coalitional arrangement that differentially incorporated blacks as minority participants would be regarded as a mark of highly effective mayoral leadership.

Seibels's ability to maintain the patterns of mayoral leadership that characterized his first six years in office will depend on the outcome of a number of developments that were taking place during his second term, perhaps the most important of which was the reawakening of black leaders to the debilitating effects of the rhetoric of progress.

Notes

1. See "Battling Bias in Steel," *Time* (December 17, 1973, p. 98; for

an interesting account of the interconnections between local government and the practices of the steel industry from the 1920s until 1951, see Hosea Hudson, *Black Worker in the Deep South* (New York: International Publishers, 1972); also see George Leighton, *Five Cities* (New York: Harpers, 1939), chapter 3.

2. This often-quoted observation was included in King's now famous "Letter from the Birmingham Jail." For the full text of the letter and a discussion of the context within which it was written, see Martin Luther King, Jr., *Why We Can't Wait* (New York: Signet Books, 1964), especially p. 78.

3. In addition to the extensive writings about and by King, there are a number of other interesting accounts of this period in Birmingham's history. Among the most useful are: Harry Holloway, *The Politics of the Southern Negro: From Exclusion to Big City Organization* (New York: Random House, 1969), especially chapter 7, "Birmingham, Alabama: Urbanism and a Politics of Race"; and, Charles Morgan, Jr., *A Time to Speak* (New York: Harper & Row, 1964).

4. See *The Government of the City of Birmingham, Alabama* (Birmingham: Office of the Mayor, May 1970).

5. Ibid.

6. An examination of Birmingham's budgets and bond issues since 1963 reveals that public works projects have absorbed nearly all the additional revenue from new taxes and bond issues. Most of the additional revenue was spent to improve the city's basic physical plant and to overcome years of decay due to neglect and indifference.

7. Holloway, *The Politics of the Southern Negro*, pp. 156-57.

8. While Townsend denied that he has been a politically powerful actor in Birmingham's affairs, nearly everyone else interviewed for this study in January 1974 referred to Townsend as the city's most influential citizen.

9. Boutwell's position toward Birmingham's racial problems was perhaps best summarized in his inaugural speech when he urged patience, restraint, and a search for harmony. In that speech he said, "It is not the purpose of the new government to serve with priority the single ambitions or hopes of any race, but to resolve the differences between them, so that they may live in peace and mutual well-being." The speech was printed in the *Birmingham News*, 21 April 1963.

10. See, "Restraint Key to Solving Problems," *Birmingham News*, 21 April 1963.

11. Interview, Birmingham, Alabama, January 7, 1974.

12. Seibels's preoccupation with the police force has often spilled over into the national media. See, for example, Leon W. Lindsay, "Birmingham

Chief Counts Accomplishments, Plunges On,'' *The Christian Science Monitor,* 25 November 1969; and Harry Wilensky, ''GOP Mayor in Birmingham Shows City's Ability to Make Major Changes,'' *St. Louis Post-Dispatch*, 4 December 1967.

13. See Roy Reed, ''Proud Birmingham Steers Into Mainstream, U.S.A.,'' *New York Times*, 28 March 1972, first page of second part and p. 74.

14. Young made a number of comments about Seibels's performance as mayor, but somehow his campaign never solidified behind a single set of issues. This quote was just one of a number of attempts by Young to capture some newsprint, since Seibels was endorsed by both major papers and was constantly in the news.

15. Scott Greenhill and Stewart Lytle, ''2 Candidates Urge Probe of Alleged ONB Fund Misuse,'' *Birmingham Post-Herald*, 27 October 1973, p. A4.

16. Ibid.

17. Interviews, Birmingham, Alabama, January 5-10, 1974.

18. See ''Is this 1963 or 1973?'' *Birmingham Post-Herald*, 27 October 1973, p. A4. Other subsequent stories in the *Post-Herald* carried lists of contributors to BAG.

19. See John Gray, ''ONB Members Censure Urged,'' *Birmingham Post-Herald,* 4 December 1973. Jefferson County commissioner Tom Gloor observed that the BAG incident was caused by ''a group of politically powerful people, comprising leadership of Operation New Birmingham and/or Birmingham Action Group coordinated these activities in a painfully amateurish fashion, without Operation New Birmingham board approval.''

20. *Operation New Birmingham Annual Report* (Birmingham: Operation New Birmingham, 1973).

21. See Carol-Faye Bruchac, ''Emphasis of Presentation on Community Affairs Committee,'' *Birmingham Post-Herald,* 10 March 1971, p. A2; and Elaine H. Miller, ''Judged by Results or Attitudes, Work of CAC is a Success,'' Ibid., p. A8.

22. Interviews, Birmingham, Alabama, January 5-10, 1974.

23. Interview, Birmingham, Alabama, January 7, 1974.

24. Ibid.

25. See notes 15, 18, and 19.

26. Interview, Birmingham, Alabama, January 7, 1974.

27. Interviews, Birmingham, Alabama, January 6, 8, 9, and 10, 1974.

28. Interviews, Birmingham, Alabama, January 6 and 8, 1974.

29. Interviews, Birmingham, Alabama, January 5-10, 1974.

30. This observation was made by a number of interviewees. Even

though the local newspapers rarely referred to the mayor's links to local business interests, this seems to be a plausible explanation for Seibels's apparent contentment with ONB/CAC activities.

31. Interviews, Birmingham, Alabama, January 5-10, 1974. The "bricks and mortar" orientation of the Seibels administration is reflected in the mayor's annual report issued each January 2 as a New Year's message.

32. Most interviewees mentioned these achievements, but not necessarily in this order.

33. See Tom Bailey, "For Our Town: Many Pluses, Some Minuses," *Birmingham News*, 31 December 1971, p. 20.

34. See Lou Isaacson, "Birmingham's Money Chief Reports City Financial Condition 'Good,'" *Birmingham News*, 25 April 1971.

35. See Scott Greenhill, "Seibels May Veto Affirmative Action Plan," *Birmingham Post-Herald*, 21 December 1973, p. B5.

36. Nearly the entire issues of the March 10, 1971 *Birmingham News* and *Post-Herald* were devoted to detailing the strategy used by the Birmingham group to "sell" the city to the All America City selection committee and to recounting the achievements of the previous eight years.

37. Birmingham's Chamber of Commerce takes great pride in pointing out that the city's white-collar employment will soon surpass its blue-collar labor force. The Chamber points to the huge University of Alabama Medical Center that is being built on fifty-four blocks of urban renewal property as indicative of the community's new economic base. See Reed, "Proud Birmingham Steering into Mainstream, U.S.A.," and the post-1967 issues of *Birmingham*, published monthly by the Birmingham Area Chamber of Commerce.

38. Interviews, Birmingham, Alabama, January 6, 7, and 10, 1974.

39. Interviews, Birmingham, Alabama, January 8, 9, and 10, 1974; also Carol Nunnelley, "Council OK's New Hiring Law," *Birmingham News*, 8 January 1974, pp. i and 9.

40. See "Discrimination Suit on Jobs Here Filed," *Birmingham News*, 8 January 1974, p. 30.

41. Interview, Birmingham, Alabama, January 10, 1974. Critics of the mayor's affirmative action veto cited a number of figures that were damaging to Seibels. For example, as of January 1, 1974, only one of Birmingham's 600 firemen was black, and of the city government's 3500 employees, only 720 were black. More significantly, of the 720 black employees working for the city, 86 percent were paid less than $6000 per year.

**Part IV
Conclusion**

7

Racial Conflict and the Future of the American Mayor: Lessons from Cleveland, Gary, and Birmingham

The case studies of racial politics in Cleveland, Gary, and Birmingham illustrate three patterns of mayoral leadership not commonly acknowledged in the literature. In each city racial cleavages presented parameters and opportunities for Mayors Stokes, Hatcher, and Seibels that influenced their behavior and their effectiveness. A number of variables implicitly used to structure the case studies are more explicitly identified in table 7-1 and are used to compare the contextual characteristics and mayoral performance in the three cities. These factors contain the major dimensions used in analyzing mayoral leadership in the three cities and cover those properties of communities considered most significant in determining mayoral effectiveness.

Contextual Characteristics

A useful way to sort out the differences between Gary, Cleveland, and Birmingham is to focus on the intensity of conflicts in the three cities and the influence of institutions and groups involved in conflict regulation and policy politics. All three cities had deep cleavages between their black and white communities that affected the politics of mayoral leadership as no other single force. Yet the cleavages between the races in each community were manifested in different ways.

Despite its reputation, Birmingham had the lowest level of conflict of the three cities from the middle sixties to the early seventies. After 1963 the city had no mass demonstrations, sit-ins, riots, or shoot-outs as the city's business elite stepped forward to guide policy making and regulate conflict. During the same period, however, Cleveland experienced several disorders and a major riot in its Hough ghetto as well as a violent shoot-out between police and black militants in 1969.

Gary falls somewhere between Birmingham and Cleveland in rancorousness. The city had no major riots or interracial shoot-outs but exceeded both cities in the personal vilification articulated by political leaders toward one another. In Gary, in contrast to Birmingham, no mediating group was willing to serve a conflict-regulating role, and the level of conflict between antagonists depended on their own self-restraint. Cleveland's business

Table 7-1
Major Contextual, Power, and Performance Dimensions of Mayoral Leadership in Cleveland, Gary, and Birmingham

Dimensions	Cleveland	Gary	Birmingham
I. Contextual Characteristics:			
A. Size	750,903	175,415	300,910
B. Interracial Relations	Polarized	Polarized	Polarized
C. Level of Overt Conflict	Sporadically Violent	Rancorous	Quiescent
D. Conflict-Mediating Influences	Weak	None	Strong
E. Black-White Power Balance	White dominated	Black dominated	White dominated
II. Mayor's Formal and Informal Power:			
A. Formal Authority	Medium	High	Low
B. Political and Managerial Expertise	Medium	Medium	Medium
III. Leadership Performance:			
A. Leadership Model	Bystander/Partisan	Partisan	Hegemonic
B. Evaluation of Leadership Effectiveness:			
1. Pluralistic Perspective	Low	Low	Medium
2. Conflict Perspective	Low/Medium	Medium/High	High

elite had a short flirtation with conflict intervention during Mayor Stokes's "Cleveland: NOW!" campaign but, like Gary's, lapsed back to indifference following the Glenville shoot-out.

In large communities conflict is normally multilateral and pluralistic.[1] However, racial polarization tends to create a dualistic pattern of interracial transactions irrespective of the size of the city. This would seem to be the case in the three cities studied. While the size of Cleveland (750,903), Birmingham (300,910), and Gary (175,415) differ, largeness did not appear to assure pluralism. But a large black population does not appear to assure rancorousness either. While Gary's population was 53.3 percent black at the time of the 1970 census, Birmingham's was 42.2 percent and Cleveland's was 39 percent. In these cities rancorous conflict between the races tended to arise more as a function of the political power of the black community rather than of its relative size compared to the size of the white population.

Intergroup relations between black and white communities tend to explain community conflict more than racial composition or community size.[2] In all three cities the social integration of blacks and whites was low; that is, blacks tended to associate almost exclusively with blacks, and whites with whites. However, the three communities did have some differences that affected racial conflict. In Gary and Cleveland the black and white communities were strongly divided at all levels by divergent goals. In Birmingham, on the other hand, the elites of the black and white community tended to share a common orientation toward local policy making. As a result, Birmingham's elites were integrated through Operation New Birmingham and the Community Affairs Committee, while in Cleveland there was only minor elite integration, and almost none in Gary. While racial politics in Gary and Cleveland tended to focus on zero-sum outcomes that would have effects at the mass level, Birmingham's politics tended to emphasize positive-sum, integrative solutions that benefited the business elite of both races, with some concessions made to improve the physical condition of both black and white neighborhoods. In Gary and Cleveland racial politics were rancorous; in Birmingham they were quiescent.

A number of other contextual characteristics shaped the structure of mayoral leadership in the three communities. In all three communities the steel industry was a major employer. Gary was primarily a one-industry town dominated by US Steel, an absentee-owned firm. Although US Steel's local managers at other times intervened in Gary's affairs, they did not play a significant role in city politics during the sixties and early seventies. Cleveland had a much higher degree of industrial pluralism than Gary, having a number of heavy industries besides steel, like oil refineries, ship building, and automobile assembly plants. Even though the owners of

Cleveland's industries resided in the suburbs, a number of local industrialists, bankers, and real estate developers maintained a substantial financial stake in the future of the city.

Birmingham, like Gary, was founded by the steel industry. However, after the early 1960s, the city's employment base moved away from a dependency on heavy industry toward white-collar industry. Even though US Steel remained the dominant employer of city residents, most of its property holdings were outside the city limits, allowing the firm to adopt an indifferent posture toward Birmingham's affairs. The presence of a successful and conservative black businessman, A.G. Gaston, contributed to the stability of relations between black and white elites and encouraged the owners and managers of the city's largest business firms to invest their time in seeking integrative solutions to Birmingham's physical problems.

While business elites can figure prominently in mediating interracial conflict, local racial radicalism can be a divisive influence.[3] This was particularly true in Cleveland, where a number of vocal black nationalist activists and organizations exacerbated white fears and antagonisms. In contrast, throughout Hatcher's first six years in office in Gary, no black radical group arose, and except for the presence of some annoying black street gangs, more inclined toward crime than radicalism, Hatcher controlled the political rhetoric and activism of the black community. In Birmingham there were neither black nationalist militancy nor black street gang activity, because much of the city's black political activism continued to be led by ministers concerned with traditional civil-rights issues.

The racial radicalism of the white communities in the three cities also differed significantly. Cleveland experienced little organized white radicalism except near elections, when racism was used as a device to mobilize white voters. Gary experienced more white extremism than Cleveland, leading to a movement among white residents of its southern area, Glen Park, to disannex the section from the city. White radicalism in Birmingham subsided after 1963, but Ku Klux Klan elements and other militant segregationists continued to advocate the use of violence to maintain white hegemony. The manifestations of white resistance to black progress in Birmingham often occurred in police practices that were, until 1972, blatantly racist and repressive.

In summary, all three cities were racially polarized, and the lines between the communities were stable and clearly drawn. Even though the black and white communities of Gary and Cleveland were better organized than in Birmingham, organizational characteristics played a smaller part in influencing overt political conflict than the commitment and activity of business elites in maintaining racial peace through intervention strategies. In Gary there were few individuals with the power or inclination to play such a mediating role, while in Cleveland there were a number of individuals with the power but few with the inclination to facilitate moderation. But in Birmingham there existed a group of people with both the power and inclination to mediate interracial conflict, and racial politics tended toward moderation.

Formal and Informal Power

The power of a mayor is a function of the formal authority provided by his office and the informal influence his background and style of leadership generate. The three case studies demonstrate how the strength or weakness of a mayoralty and individual mayor facilitate or limit the capacity of a mayor to lead. Comparing the power of Stokes, Hatcher, and Seibels is difficult, since Seibels's goals seem to better fit the prevailing power structure in Birmingham. Even so, the formal authority of the mayoralty in the three cities contributed significantly to the ability of the mayor to exercise influence.

Gary provides its mayor with many formal powers: he can hire and fire department heads, he appoints the members of most of the important boards and commissions, has a four-year term, and is elected along with the city council in partisan elections. Cleveland's mayor has less formal authority than Gary's. He can hire and fire department heads, but many boards and commissions are independently elected, and he must stand for reelection every two years along with Cleveland's thirty-three councilmen, who are elected by wards, making mayoral attempts at party leadership unfeasible. In Birmingham the mayor's role is even weaker. The city's mayor cannot hire or fire department heads at will, because they are protected by the county's powerful civil-service system. In addition, the mayor does not influence the election of the city's nine councilmen, who are elected in nonpartisan, at-large contests and who control appointments to most of the city's boards and commissions.

But even if the mayors' powers in Birmingham, Gary, and Cleveland were comparable, the skills and ambitions of Seibels, Stokes, and Hatcher would probably have produced patterns of leadership effectiveness similar to those they produced during their first two terms in office. During his first year in office, Stokes attempted to forge an executive-centered biracial coalition, but after the Glenville shoot-out, he became a bystander. During his second term, with his political career seemingly at an end, he adopted a more racially partisan posture to salvage at least symbolic recompense from his stagnated and frustrating incumbency. As the most influential member of a predominantly black coalition in a white-dominated city, Stokes relied on his public relations skills, his standing as a Democrat, his extensive political experience, and his reputation as a racial moderate in his initial attempts to build a biracial coalition in Cleveland. However, once he began to articulate partisan positions on issues, much of the goodwill he had accumulated in the white community quickly evaporated.

Seibels's style was similar to Stokes's. Like Stokes and Hatcher, he had no experience managing large-scale organizations before taking office and had difficulties adjusting to the demands of controlling a large budget and a complex bureaucracy. Seibels was a Republican, but Birmingham's nonpartisan electoral system allowed him to avoid identification with his party. The Mayor's ability to minimize racial conflict was enhanced by his low commitment to racial partisanship and his activist style, but his lack of tolerance for criticism of his administration and his resistance of proposals to have the city government launch programs aimed specifically at enhancing black economic development led black and white liberals to become disenchanted with his leadership. Because Seibels was a secondary leader of a white-controlled dominant coalition and shared the coalition's basic goals for Birmingham's development, he was a successful partner in a hegemonic regime, not an innovative civic entrepreneur.

In comparison to the extroverted leadership styles of Stokes and Seibels, Richard Hatcher tended to be an introvert. Because the major local newspaper and most of the white community was hostile or indifferent to his administration, Hatcher concentrated his attention on quietly consolidating black power in Gary and attracting federal and foundation funds to the city. Hatcher had a high commitment to encouraging black political and economic progress and was unwilling to sacrifice these goals by compromising with white interests. His partisan leadership style neatly fit his role as the leader of Gary's dominant black coalition.

Effectiveness and Policy Impact

By approaching the study of mayoral leadership with "paired models" of situational contexts—the polarized city and the pluralized city—this study has sought to avoid the bias of interpreting urban politics solely through the "lens" of the pluralist model.[4] Instead, a conflict framework has been introduced and used to interpret the impressionistic evidence presented in the three case studies, a perspective that better "fits" the contemporary realities of community politics in many American cities.

Through the use of a conflict model, the evaluation of the leadership performances of Stokes, Hatcher, and Seibels changed dramatically. From a pluralist perspective, Richard Hatcher's leadership structure and policy achievements would merit low effectiveness scores, even though he centralized politics in the mayoralty. His failure to integrate black and white interests, to mobilize both communities in Gary, and to develop a series of overarching policy and program changes would be considered signs of ineffective leadership. However, an evaluation from a conflict perspective would give him a much higher leadership rating. Because Gary's blacks were Hatcher's primary constituents, the mayor's ability to integrate and dominate black politics, to mobilize the black community, to distribute numerous political rewards almost exclusively to the black community, and to initiate a number of innovative programs aimed at Gary's blacks would give him a much higher effectiveness rating than an evaluation in terms of the pluralist model of mayoral leadership.

Similarly, Carl Stokes's performance would be evaluated more highly from a conflict than from a pluralist perspective. From a pluralist perspective, the mayor's failure to maintain the executive-centered coalition that he built around "Cleveland: NOW!" during his first term would be considered a mark of failure. However, a conflict perspective would regard his ability to mobilize the black community, help establish the 21st Congressional District Caucus, and distribute some political rewards solely to the black community as indicators of a more effective leadership performance than would be acknowledged by a pluralist analysis.

George Seibels's performance in Birmingham presented an even more subtle distinction, since he was a secondary leader in a white hegemonic coalition. Through adroit public relations efforts, Seibels helped persuade Birmingham's blacks to support programs aimed at improving the city's physical condition at a high opportunity cost to black-oriented social welfare programs. From a pluralist perspective, Seibels's performance would rate higher than Stokes's or Hatcher's, because substantial change was achieved during his mayoralty, even though Seibels never centralized, or integrated politics around the mayoralty. In many ways, Seibels was more of a follower of the city's powerful business interests than a leader in policy formation. On the other hand, a conflict perspective would view Seibels's mayoral performance as far more effective. Because Birmingham's politics were dominated by a white hegemony, Seibels's role was to maintain the city's power and policy status quo. To do this, Birmingham's city government granted the black community some token concessions and pursued a massive public works program that could be defended as benefiting both blacks and whites. Through this strategy, Seibels was able to transfer a heavy opportunity cost to Birmingham's black community without arousing its anger. Therefore, while Stokes and Hatcher used the symbolism of black progress and power to build their own strengths and to keep the black community mobilized, Seibels used the symbolism of communitywide progress to keep the black community quiescent and fragmented.

Racial Conflict and the Future of the American Mayoralty

People enter political life for a variety of reasons: to enhance their power and prestige, to serve their community, to advance to higher office, to improve the quality of life in their community, to reform governmental operations, or simply to have something to occupy their time.[5] Although the American mayoralty has been a political "dead end" for career politicians since World War II, it nevertheless has provided a vehicle for people commited to civic improvement to initiate and implement changes in the social, political, and ecological fabrics of their communities.[6] Since the mid-sixties, however, the growth of black populations and racial consciousness has created new forces in urban politics, preventing many urban mayors from deriving the personal satisfaction of activating even minimal levels of change in their communities. The potential long-range effects of polarization on the office of mayor are difficult to predict, but four possible outcomes seem particularly significant for the future: (1) more blacks will be elected to the mayorships of large and medium-size cities; (2) more city governments will be immobilized by polarization; (3) more cities will have hegemonic regimes; and (4) the federal government will reassert its influence in local affairs. Although the following analysis is largely speculative, the problem of polarization is sufficiently serious to warrant forecasting even if it can only be undertaken in this study on a cursory basis.

Black Mayors

Making predictions from data on past trends is usually hazardous, but in the case of blacks capturing urban mayoralties, the future seems assured. Since the mid-sixties blacks have been elected to the office of mayor at an exponential rate. In 1969 there were only 29 black mayors in the United States and only two, Stokes and Hatcher, served in large cities. But by February 1973, there were 82 black mayors, and their numbers increased to 107 by 1974. Further, during the period from 1969 to 1974, black mayors took office in big cities like Atlanta, Detroit, Los Angeles, and Newark as well as in a number of smaller cities like Raleigh, North Carolina; Dayton, Ohio; East St. Louis, Illinois; and East Orange, New Jersey.

In many of the cities where blacks have been elected mayor, blacks comprise a majority or near majority of the population. In other communities, like Dayton (30.5 percent), Cleveland (38.3 percent), and Pontiac, Michigan (26.7 percent), blacks comprise a sizable percentage of the population. In still other communities where the mayoralty is largely a symbolic and ceremonial position, black councilmen have been elected by their fellow city councilmen to serve limited terms. This phenomena has occurred in a number of council-manager cities with large liberal communities like the university towns of Boulder, Colorado, and New Brunswick, New Jersey. Despite the apparent negation of the polarization argument by these exceptions and the presence of a black mayor in Los

Angeles, a city with only 17.9 percent of its population black, in nearly every election involving major black and white candidates, black voters have voted as a bloc with between 95 and 99 percent of their votes going to the black candidate. Likewise, in most cases, black candidates have been unable to capture more than 25 percent of the white vote.[7] This voting pattern highlights the importance of population composition to the political opportunity structure of black politicians and suggests that in the future black-versus-white elections will continue to be contests of demographics.

Table 7-2 presents those mayor-council cities of over 50,000 where more than 35 percent of the population was black at the time of the 1970 census. Because blacks tend to vote in blocs for black candidates in biracial elections, these are the American cities most likely to elect black mayors. The table categorizes the cities by region and size. The regional distinction was made because black political participation in the South has generally lagged behind the rest of the country. The size distinction was made to isolate the effects of city size on black political organization.

Table 7-2 shows that outside of the South, four of the six cities with over 45 percent of the population black had black mayors in February 1974. The one major exception, Baltimore, had an intense political rivalry between two black political factions throughout the late sixties and early seventies which retarded the development of black political power.[8]

The South, however, presents a very different picture. Even though Raleigh and Atlanta elected black mayors in 1973, blacks have failed to mount viable mayoral campaigns in Augusta, Charleston, Birmingham, and New Orleans, where they constitute a near majority. If population trends continue, it will be only a short time before these cities become predominantly black. Meanwhile, changes in southern industrial development should lead to the lessening of black dependence on white-owned, locally controlled industry and agriculture, allowing blacks more freedom to organize and eventually to outvote whites.[9] The election of black mayors in the South, while temporarily stalled in smaller cities by economic dependence and organizational ineffectiveness, is inevitable.

The contest of demographics that characterize black-versus-white electoral contests tends to be obscured by exceptions like Los Angeles. Yet, in city after city, polarized election results emerge. This pattern has persisted in elections in Gary, Cleveland, Newark, Atlanta, and Detroit, and even though some blacks will be elected when the numbers are not "right," the calculation of political opportunity for black politicians will continue for a number of years ahead to rely on the statistics of racial composition.[10]

Immobilism

Even if blacks capture more mayoralties, there is no guarantee that they

Table 7-2
Mayor-Council Cities of Over 50,000 with More Than 35 Percent of Population Black

Population	NONSOUTHERN CITIES			SOUTHERN CITIES		
	35-39.9 Percent	*40-44.9 Percent*	*45 Percent and over*	*35-39.9 Percent*	*40-44.9 Percent*	*45 Percent and over*
50,000 to 150,000	Mount Vernon, N.Y. (72,778; 35.6%) Camden, N.J. (102,551; 39.1%) Trenton, N.J. (104,638; 37.9%)	Wilmington, Del. (80,368; 43.6%)	Chester, Pa. (56,331; 45.2%) East St. Louis, Ill. (69,996; 69.1%)[a] East Orange, N.Y. (75,471; 53.1%)[a]	Monroe, La. (56,374; 38.2%) Albany, Ga. (72,623; 37.9%) Macon, Ga. (122,423; 37.3%)	Pine Bluff, Ark. (57,389; 40.9%)	Augusta, Ga. (59,864; 49.9%) Charleston, S.C. (66,945; 45.1%)
150,000 to 400,000			Gary, Ind. (175,415; 52.8%)[a] Newark, N.J. (382,417; 54.2%)[a]		Birmingham, Ala. (300,910; 42.0%)	
400,000 and over	Cleveland, Ohio (750,903; 38.3%)[a]	St. Louis, Mo. (622,236; 40.8%) Detroit, Mich. (1,511,482; 43.7%)[a]	Baltimore, Md. (905,759; 46.4%)	Memphis, Tenn. (623,530; 38.9%)		Atlanta, Ga. (496,973; 51.3%)[a] New Orleans, La. (593,471; 45.0%)

[a]City has or has had a black mayor

will have more success than their white counterparts at influencing the future of their cities. Variations in urban service distribution and mayoral partisanship are accurately perceived and translated into attitudes about local government by black and white citizens.[11] In a study of attitudes toward city government using data originally gathered from fifteen cities in 1968 as part of the supplemental studies to the Kerner Commission Report, Schuman and Gruenberg found that when a mayor was more popular with one race, he was less so with the other.[12] Thus, while blacks held favorable attitudes toward Carl Stokes, Richard Hatcher, and Walter Washington (the appointed mayor of Washington, D.C.) and the white liberal mayors of San Francisco, Boston, and Baltimore, they were less pleased with the performances of Henry Maier of Milwaukee and Richard Daley of Chicago. Whites, on the other hand, were favorable toward Maier and Daley, held favorable or at least neutral attitudes toward the mayors of Boston, Baltimore, San Francisco, and Washington, D.C., joined with blacks in negatively reacting to Hugh Addonisio in Newark, and were less favorable toward Stokes and Hatcher than blacks.

Schuman and Gruenberg conclude that the level of confidence in the mayor of a city may constitute a useful indicator of the more general level of trust citizens have in the rest of the city government, and that the trust or confidence blacks and whites express toward local government is at least partially racial in content. "This interpretation also is congruent with the fact that the two cities with the highest levels of [black] dissatisfaction involve mayors probably perceived in 1968 as more representative of whites than of blacks, while three of the four cities at the other extreme had Negro mayors in 1968."[13]

Because blacks and whites are sensitive to the racial partisanship of local government and the mayor, their political responses to mayoral leadership efforts will tend to reflect racial considerations. Yet blacks will tend to pay more heed to local government than whites and will tend to react with more intensity to the partisanship of a white mayor than whites toward the partisanship of a black mayor. A speculative but persuasive explanation for this phenomena has been offered by Rossi and Berk:

It may be symbolically important to blacks to have one of their race as mayor, but it is also important in other respects that whatever mayor is in office make efforts to improve the position of blacks *vis-à-vis* local municipal institutions. With the data on hand, we can only speculate as to the reasons for this sensitivity. Obviously the location choices for blacks play some role: If you can't move from the central city because of restrictions arising from discrimination and low income levels, then what goes on in the central city's mayor's office is more salient. It may also be the case that more of the total real income of blacks is provided in the form of municipal services. In other words, if you are poor and black, it is more important to you that the public schools be of reasonable quality, that the police treat you with respect and provide protection and aid, etc., because you have little discretionary income and power to provide such services from alternative sources or to compensate in other ways for their absence.[14]

The relative importance of local services to black residents means that black demands for services will rise as the black population grows. At the same time, whites will resist any redistribution of services or increases in local taxes, since their stake in remaining in the city is in part contingent on the relatively lower cost of housing and taxation in the city than in the suburbs. Polarization will undoubtedly arise even in those cities that were relatively unscathed by ghetto rioting in the sixties. Many city governments, caught in the conflict of expectations between blacks and whites, will slide into immobilism.

The solution most often proposed to resolve the immobilized politics of American urban race relations is the biracial consociation of elites that works with the mayor to build integrative solutions for local problems. But the consociational strategy works best when both groups are stable and have an equal stake in the future of the community. As long as the black population continues to grow and whites yearn for the day they can exit to the suburbs, their perceived commitment in the future of the central city will differ.[15] Likewise, black dependency on local government services will lead to more pressure for better services and jobs and, consequently, higher taxes, making compromise solutions difficult if not impossible to achieve.

Even though the American mayoralty seems destined to bring little but frustration to incumbents, there are two alternatives to urban political immobilism, and both involve the mayor in a critical role. The first alternative, hegemony, will unquestionably arise in some communities as an answer to immobilism. The second, a "vertical" coalition of local government with agencies of the federal government is more problematic.

Hegemony

Extraordinary political leaders tend to appear in times of extraordinary political conflict. Although the office of mayor normally does not provide opportunities for charismatic leadership, in conflict-torn communities a mayor may have the opportunity to define issues in a manner that will capture the aspirations of his racial group and mobilize them to solidify their hold on city government to reap a disproportionate share of city jobs and services. In polarized communities, domination becomes the most salient political goal, and the hegemony of one group over the other is a likely outcome.[16]

The use of charismatic appeals by a mayor-leader may provide him with inexpensive and flexible resources to exchange for support and give him political leverage out of proportion to his formal authority.[17] For example, by mobilizing community interest in governmental operations, a mayor can use citizen groups as counterweights to the power of the bureaucracies because "they constitute an alternative channel of information about administrative performance, reducing executive dependence on the bureaucracies on the one hand and on the mass media (with their bias toward the sensational) on the other."[18]

The mobilization of racial communities to control a city government requires that a solid majority must be on hand and activated. Despite the difficulties involved in mobilizing a community to control a city government, the domination of a city government by one ethnic or racial group has occurred and continues to be possible within the prevailing rules of city politics.

As black political power increases through population growth and political mobilization, black mayors may be persuaded to adopt racially partisan postures to improve the living conditions of their black constituents. As stable black majorities form in more localities and some city governments come under firm black control, black mayors may be able to build winning coalitions powerful enough to implement major change without consulting whites, that is, to build racially exclusive hegemonic regimes.

While the process of black political consolidation is occurring, whites will flee the city, hastening the pace of black control and setting the stage for the final phase in the evolution of black mayoral leadership: the creation of executive-centered coalitions within black political systems. As cities become more firmly controlled by blacks and the importance of appeals to racial pride diminish, a pluralism of different interests within the black conmunity based on class, location, and special interest is likely to emerge. In this system black mayors will be elected who are capable of brokering, consolidating, and molding the various community interests into black-dominated, executive-centered coalitions.

As the number and power of black mayors increase, efforts will be made to co-opt their militancy. In order to convince black leaders that their communities will be better off if they pursue cooperative rather than combative strategies, mediating parties will have to marshal vast amounts of financial incentives. Since white-owned businesses and industries will abandon the central city if their taxes are increased, the only available sources of funds for new programs to combat urban problems will lie outside the central city in the budgets of federal agencies. Because the interest of the federal government in urban problems has waned in the early seventies, a renewal of its commitment to improve urban life will be required to forestall racial hegemony or immobilism in the cities of the near future.

The Reassertion of Federal Influence

The 1960s witnessed the beginnings of a new approach to attacking urban problems. Before the "Great Society" programs of the Johnson administration, the standard response to urban decay involved the physical renewal of the core cities and the reform of municipal organizational arrangements to foster more efficient delivery of municipal services. During the 1960s, however, policy-makers began to realize that the reform of institutional arrangements and the physical rebuilding of core cities could not alone solve urban problems. Instead, programs were begun in a number of communities aimed at improving the social and economic condition of the urban poor. These programs were conceived and initiated by coalitions that integrated local governmental agencies, community service organizations, federal agencies, and private foundations. Many of the more ambitious urban social programs and effective coalitions were conceived and activated by skillful and imaginative white liberal mayors who rose to national prominence as the saviors of their cities. But by the late sixties, programs aimed at combating urban (and mostly black) poverty-related problems conflicted with the preferences of most of the liberal mayors' white constituents, bringing the political careers of many white liberal mayors to an end.[19]

At the same time that white liberal mayors were leaving office, the Nixon administration began to disengage the federal government from its overt involvement with local efforts to attack urban problems, relying more heavily on revenue sharing rather than special-purpose grants-in-aid to provide slack resources for local problem solving. While the intent of the "New Federalism" is difficult to discern, at least part of the disengagement strategy was intended to preserve local spending options and have programming better reflect prevailing local power alignments and policy preferences. But the racial polarization and concomitant political immobilism of many cities made the Nixon administration's model for solving urban problems unfeasible, because the "horizontal" coalition of local individuals, interest groups, and institutions that was expected to accurately reflect local policy preferences could not be molded or maintained in communities where racial consciousness and conflict were high.

Yet the financial involvement of the federal government is critical if urban and especially black urban problems are ever to be alleviated and if mayors are ever expected to effectively lead their city's attacks on urban poverty problems. When a mayor receives outside funds, he can provide leadership for his city even though he does not command all the political resources and policy-making authority usually associated with strong mayoral leadership.

Of the three cases presented in this study, the "vertical" model was more effective in Gary than in Cleveland or Birmingham. However, in all three cities, the involvement of the federal government figured prominently in bringing about change and relieving the debilitating effects of immobilism on mayoral leadership. In Gary and, to a lesser degree, in Cleveland, the availability of federal funds lessened the necessity of Mayors Hatcher and Stokes to build locally based leadership structures. Since the success of their leadership efforts did not conform very closely to their communities' power structures, Hatcher and Stokes were freed from dealing with the veto powers of local antagonists. However, as the novelty of their status as America's first black big city mayors diminished and the Nixon administration readjusted federal priorities to limit slack resources for urban programming, the abilities of Hatcher and Stokes to generate outside funds declined. When that happened, their impact became more congruent with their local leadership structure, and the pattern of conflict in the community became more salient for policy making than in their first two or three years in office.

Black mayors are under great pressure to choose between adapting militant postures to dispense symbolic rewards to their black constituents while a long-term black power base is being formed or allowing themselves to be co-opted by federal and foundation funds in order to attack substantive problems.[20] But the federal government also has a strategic choice. If its financial contributions to urban governments only provide palliatives where major changes are needed, one can expect future black city governments to become increasingly militant. If, however, the reassertion of federal influence in city affairs is accompanied by meaningful financial aid, black mayors can be expected to adopt more moderate postures. In the future, no matter what party controls federal policy, the level of federal involvement in local problems will become a strategic device for mediating and moderating the politics of race in America's cities.

The alternative to either hegemony or federal involvement in polarized communities may ultimately be a crippling of the American mayoralty. If the racial polarization of American cities produces a political situation that makes it impossible for any elected mayor—black or white—to accomplish any significant improvement, then men of enthusiasm, ambition, and imagination will refuse to seek the office and our cities will lose their critically needed services. If it is determined conclusively, as is argued in this study, that the problems of effective executive leadership in cities is a structural problem and not a personal deficiency of the people recruited to the mayoralty, then our expectations for aggressive mayoral leadership must change and our search for solutions to urban problems must look for other sources of initiative and other forms of local government.

Notes

1. See Terry Nichols Clark, *Community Power and Policy Outputs: A Review of Urban Research* (Beverly Hills, Calif.: Sage Publications, 1973), pp. 31-34.

2. For a discussion of the importance of intergroup relations in facilitating overt conflict or quiescence, see Leo Kuper, "Plural Societies: Perspectives and Problems," in Leo Kuper and M.G. Smith (eds.) *Pluralism in Africa* (Berkeley, Calif.: University of California Press, 1969).

3. The divisive effects of radical nationalism is perhaps best exemplified by the impact of the activities of Protestant and Catholic extremist groups in Northern Ireland. See Richard Rose, *Governing Without Consensus: An Irish Perspective* (Boston: The Beacon Press, 1971).

4. For a discussion of the importance of "paired models" in leadership studies, see Donald D. Searing, "Models and Images of Man and Society in Leadership Theory," *Journal of Politics* 31 (February 1969), pp. 3-31, especially pp. 26-31.

5. For a discussion of the motives that draw people into urban politics, see Charles R. Adrian, "The Quality of Urban Leadership" in Henry J. Schmandt and Warner Bloomberg, Jr. (eds.) *The Quality of Urban Life* (Beverly Hills, Calif.: Sage Publications, 1969), pp. 375-93.

6. See Marilyn Gittell, "Metropolitan Mayor: Dead End," *Public Administration Review,* 23 (March 1963), pp. 20-24.

7. See Charles H. Levine, "Community Conflict and Mayoral Leadership," unpublished Ph.D. dissertation, Indiana University, 1971, pp. 461-64.

8. See G. James Fleming, *Baltimore's Failure to Elect a Black Mayor in 1971* (Washington, D.C.: Joint Center for Political Studies, 1972).

9. For an analysis of the crippling effects of fear and economic dependency on black political participation in the Deep South, see Lester M. Salamon and Stephen Van Evera, "Fear, Apathy, and Discrimination: A Test of Three Explanations of Political Participation," *American Political Science Review* 67 (December 1973), pp. 1288-1306.

10. See Chuck Stone, *Black Political Power in America,* revised edition (New York: Dell Publishing Co., 1970), pp. 229-30 for a list of "ingredients" necessary for black candidates to win mayoral elections.

11. See Howard Schuman and Barry Gruenberg, "The Impact of City on Racial Attitudes," *American Journal of Sociology* 76 (September 1970), (copyright © 1970 by University of Chicago Press), pp. 213-61; and Peter H. Rossi and Richard A. Berk, "Generalized Performance Measures for Urban Political Systems," a paper prepared for the 69th Annual Meeting of

the American Political Science Association, New Orleans, Louisiana, September 4-8, 1973.

12. Schuman and Gruenberg, "The Impact of City on Racial Attitudes," p. 236.

13. Ibid., p. 241.

14. Rossi and Berk, "Generalized Performance Measures for Urban Political Systems," p. 31.

15. See John M. Orbell and Toru Uno, "A Theory of Neighborhood Problem Solving: Political Action vs. Residential Mobility," *American Political Science Review* 66 (June 1972), pp. 471-89.

16. See Ann Ruth Willner and Dorothy Willner, "The Rise and Role of Charismatic Leaders," Annals of the American Academy of Political and Social Science (March 1965), pp. 77-88; also Murray Edelman, "Escalation and Ritualization of Political Conflict," *American Behavioral Scientist* 13 (November/December 1969), pp. 231-46.

17. See Robert C. Tucker, "The Theory of Charismatic Leadership," *Daedalus* 97 (Summer 1968), pp. 731-56.

18. Herbert Kaufman, "Administrative Decentralization and Political Power," *Public Administration Review* 29 (January/February 1960), p. 11.

19. See James Q. Wilson, "The Mayors vs. the Cities," *Public Interest* 16 (Summer 1969), pp. 25-40.

20. See Edward Greer, "The Liberation of Gary, Indiana," *Trans-action* 8 (January 1971), p. 63.

**Toward a Contingency
Theory of Mayoral
Effectiveness**

The folly of searching for a single factor to explain leadership effectiveness has become a well-accepted dictum of leadership research.[1] Years of research and debate have finally produced a consensus among students of leadership that theories based solely on either traits, styles, or situations have failed to account for significant variations in executive behavior, performance, and effectiveness. Within the field of management, it has become increasingly well accepted that leadership effectiveness is contingent upon the interaction of certain properties of a manager's behavioral style with specific characteristics of his task environment. Through the development of contingency theories of leadership effectiveness, students of leadership have begun to better understand the complex nature of these interrelationships and have begun to build linkages between behavioral studies of management and management science.

The contingency approach is a departure from previous leadership research because it explicitly assumes that there is no "one best way" or style that produces effective outcomes. Instead, contingency theorists assume: (1) that different leadership styles produce more or less effective outcomes in different contexts; (2) that situations vary in their responsiveness or favorableness to leadership initiatives; and (3) that certain leadership styles will better "fit" specific situations than others.[2] Moving from these three assumptions to a contingency theory requires: (1) determining which situational variables should be considered relevant and how they should be operationalized and weighed; (2) identifying and operationalizing leadership styles, i.e., behavioral orientations; and (3) developing multidimensional measures of effectiveness. Since style and situation interact to coproduce a leadership performance, a contingency theory should explain why a performance failed or succeeded. It should also allow an analyst to recommend changes in style or context based on empirically informed knowledge of the styles that better "fit" specific contexts. In short, a well-developed contingency theory allows the analyst to predict which situations are most likely to be effected by leadership initiatives, which situations are most likely to produce frustration, and given an individual with a dominant leadership style, his relative effectiveness in a number of different contexts.

The contingency approach is particularly well suited for urban political research, because variations in urban contexts shape the effectiveness of the leadership styles used by urban executives. Understanding the interaction effects and outcomes produced when particular styles and situations are juxtaposed in urban settings is an important and useful focus, because it stresses the linkages between patterns of political behavior, social structures, and outcomes. This theoretical thrust is consistent with the contemporary development of political science that for the past two decades has aimed at untangling the complexity associated with "behavior-structure-outcome" relationships.

The "behavior-structure-outcome" focus is important for the development of political science, because knowledge tends to be accumulated about parts of a system before it is gathered about the interfaces between the parts. The contingency approach stresses the relational characteristics among subsystems and suggests the parts of a system that are informationally overdeveloped and those parts that are in need of greater attention. It also suggests to the researcher linkages to be explored and the interaction effects that are likely to produce significant theoretical breakthroughs.

Fragmented and unrelated knowledge about subsystems frustrates the development of both theory building and strategic design. This has been particularly true in the narrow subfield of mayoral leadership, where case studies of elements of leadership systems have provided descriptive knowledge but little empirical theory. To overcome the lack of theory about urban political leadership and to provide urban executives with useful leadership strategies, political scientists must begin to embrace integrative frameworks for explaining leadership phenomena that stress relational properties of leadership systems and sort out irrelevant units and levels of analysis. The recent development of contingency theories in the field of organizational behavior provides a promising direction for integrating our knowledge about mayoral leadership and for the development of theory-informed action strategies for more effective mayoral performance.

The contingency approach promises a great deal, but the development of contingency models is a complicated and demanding scientific undertaking. Even Fred E. Fiedler's work, to date the most advanced and exhaustive effort to develop a contingency theory of leadership effectiveness, has been severely criticized on methodological grounds.[3] Predicting from available contingency models is hazardous, and the techniques used for operationalizing situational variables and situational favorableness has left contingency research open to charges of "post-hoc ordering of data buttressed by convoluted justifications."[4] But even if these problems did not exist, the direction of prevailing research trends in political science would appear to indicate that the prospects for contingency modeling by political scientists are only fair. Despite the consistency of the contingency approach with prevailing trends in political research, the sociology of the discipline and the implications of contingency research are in dramatic conflict, making the case for adoption of contingency modeling by political scientists less than self-evident.

The Sociology of Political Knowledge and the Administrative Science of Mayoral Leadership

The study of executive performance is divided into two almost mutually exclusive orientations: administrative behavior and administrative science. The two modes of analysis differ in intent and aspiration.[5] The study of administrative behavior involves the development of abstract theories of *why* executives behave the way they do and *why* differences in behavior produce different outcomes. Administrative science, on the other hand, is oriented toward developing models of *how* to produce desired outcomes. Behavioral scientists are committed to theory building within a positivist paradigm and use abstract variables in their theories, irrespective of their controllability in the real world. In contrast, management scientists seek to design action strategies within an operational framework and concentrate on variables in the natural world that are amenable to control. In the field of political science, the development of a behavioral science of executive performance is now well under way, but efforts to use these theories to predict outcomes or design action strategies for political executives have been less impressive. The recent development of contingency theories and a metatheory for the "science of design" offer hope that the gap between the study of administrative behavior and administrative science can eventually be bridged.

If there are great potential theoretical and utilitarian payoffs for unifying the fields of administrative behavior and administrative science, why haven't the two orientations already been linked? The explanation lies in the sociology of political knowledge, in the behavioral dynamics of the discipline of political science that have produced a detachment from the real world of politics and a conservatism toward prediction; both trends lead away rather than toward a unification of behavioral political science with a science of political design.

During the past three decades, political scientists have adopted the behavioral approach in an effort to make political knowledge more scientific and the discipline more academically respectable. The thrust toward a more technically sophisticated science of politics has led scholars away from the world of political practice and into the realm of advanced statistics, methodology, and computer processing. The use of unobtrusive measures, mass surveys, and aggregate data analysis (sometimes of hundreds of political units in the same study) has allowed political scientists to generalize about political systems without any face-to-face familiarity with their principal actors or internal dynamics. Within the discipline this refining of concepts and methodologies is justified by the argument that the purpose of political science is to gain "knowledge for knowledge sake" and that some day these efforts will provide pragmatically valuable knowledge for practitioners.

Students of political leadership share this detached orientation with the rest of political science, but their withdrawal from pragmatic research has been even more exaggerated by their fragmentation and self-imposed isolation from other disciplines. Within political science, the study of leadership has been fragmented into a number of separate subfields and research thrusts, each accompanied by methodological and theoretical debates.[6] Within each sector of the subfield, scholars tend to specialize in a single issue, individual, area, or office. It is not unusual in leadership research to find specialists on issues like the methodology of community power studies; on offices like the mayoralty and the presidency; on areas like individual cities, states, and nations; or on individuals like Mayor Hatcher, while being almost totally oblivious to the importance of their work to the wider stream of research on leadership.

Because political scientists have been preoccupied with developing their own theories, they have missed the trends of research within related disciplines, preventing a cross fertilization of methodology and theory. In particular, by ignoring recent developments in leadership research within the fields of management and social psychology, political scientists have missed opportunities to adopt new approaches to their traditional concerns. If they had been paying closer attention to these other fields, political scientists might have discovered methods to integrate their fragmented concerns and develop more generalizable propositions.

If political science approaches to leadership can be accused of lacking focus, then the study of urban leadership must be considered inchoate. The American study of urban politics has no separate theoretical justification. The four major research trends in the field—institutional reform, community power, protest behavior, and public policy—are all outgrowths of wider concerns that are equally relevant to other levels of government. The unique properties of urbanization, such as high density, high interaction, specialization of function, and spatial competition are rarely systematically incorporated in theories of urban politics. Even the phenomena of urban racial politics has rarely been approached as a product of the unique functions of urban areas. Lacking a separate theoretical focus, students of urban leadership spent most of the 1960s addressing their research to questions of democratic theory and associated methodological controversies: "Who governs?" and "What difference does it make?"

Even when students of urban leadership wanted to move beyond questions of democratic theory and methodology to address themselves to more pragmatic questions ("how to govern" and "how to govern effectively"), they found the field of political science lacking a guiding, action-oriented framework. Previous studies of urban leadership often went no further than to describe leadership as a process of exchange and integration, failing to deal with the impact of urban settings on leadership performance or the complex problem of measuring leadership effectiveness. The analysis of urban leaders in the 1960s was often journalistic and atheoretical. There never developed a concerted effort to build a framework for analysis that might some day evolve into an administrative science for effectively performing urban leadership roles.

Despite this gloomy picture, political science does have some unique traditions that provide the opportunity for scholars to contribute to a management science of urban leadership. The discipline does not have exclusive rights to studying power nor does it monopolize academic concerns with "the authoritative allocation of values." Instead, the strength of political science lies in its traditional concern for the formal institutions of politics. For decades political scientists have been accumulating knowledge about the roles, rules, and processes of institutions like the mayoralty, nonpartisan elections, and the executive veto, to mention just a few examples. Using comparative analysis and adopting approaches from other fields, students of politics could exploit their base of institutional expertise to build both better theories and a management science of political leadership.

The evolution of a science of mayoral leadership from description and classification to explanation and prescription is constrained by the present state of our knowledge. Available descriptions of mayoral behavior are partial, static, and superficial at best. We need to know more about what mayors actually do and the processes they use to manage their work-flow and to accomplish their objectives.[7] We also need to develop classifications that are mutually exclusive and exhaustive. At present, the few typologies of mayoral leadership that have been developed do not meet these standards. Finally, we need to form our research interests with greater attention to what mayors need to know, so they can better develop strategic designs and make more intelligent choices. A management science of mayoral leadership requires a departure from past and present patterns of accumulating political knowledge. It requires a choice and action orientation; otherwise, the best political science can ever provide are explanations *why* things go right or wrong. By continuing our present orientation, we will never provide strategies for *how* to make things go right!

A Hypothetical Contingency Theory of Mayoral Leadership

A contingency theory of mayoral leadership can serve as a bridge between theory construction and strategic design. Because contingency theories sort behavioral styles and organizational structures into categories that are more or less effective in discrete situations, they can also be used for predictive and action purposes. Contingency research, therefore, serves two purposes: action explanation and action prescription. This dual orientation makes contingency research different from earlier trends in behavioral research and offers hope that the false dichotomy between theory building and political/administrative practice will eventually disappear.

The development of contingency theories of leadership requires the construction of multidimensional indexes of situations, styles, and effectiveness. Eventually, the construction of these indexes will be based on the selection of variables that are found to have the greatest explanatory power; but initially, in the preliminary stages of research, salient variables can be derived from reviewing previous research in the field.

The total number of variables in a contingency theory of leadership will not be excessively large, because leadership systems can be treated as *nearly decomposable* systems.[8] In a nearly decomposable system, Simon argues, "the short-run behavior of each of the component subsystems is approximately independent of the short-run behavior of the other components"; but "in the long run, the behavior of any one of the components depends in only an aggregate way on the behavior of the other components."[9] Therefore, a contingency theory of mayoral effectiveness need not stipulate every interaction among parts of a subsystem or between systems, but can instead concentrate on explaining the gross interaction effects of the two major subsystems, in this case, style and situation.

Aggregating interactions between the subsystems of nearly decomposable systems simplifies the task of constructing contingency theories. By drawing upon previous research to construct a tentative contingency theory of mayoral leadership effectiveness, hypotheses can be formed that can be eventually tested and modified. Because of its relatively simple format, a contingency model can also be easily communicated to the practitioner who might use the theory to strategize. Because of these properties, a carefully constructed and tested contingency theory of mayoral leadership can be a major contribution to both theory and practice.

Situational Factors

In studies of mayoral leadership, three properties of a mayor's task environment—interorganizational relations, task structure, and position power—have been stressed and therefore should be initially incorporated in a hypothetical contingency theory. For the purposes of this discussion, these three factors will only be briefly sketched.

A community's *interorganizational relations* include the degree to which members of the community are organized into formal and informal groups, the degree that they share cross-cutting memberships, the degree of rancorousness in conflictual behavior, and the degree of stability in conflictual and cooperative relations.[10] These are just four of the more salient characteristics of interorganizational relations within communities. Other factors may undoubtedly warrant inclusion, but with these four factors, communities can be characterized as varying between pluralistic and polarized. Pluralistic communities are hypothesized to be more favorable to mayoral leadership initiatives than polarized communities.

A mayor's *task structure* is composed of the problems he faces and their characteristics. More specifically, tasks are relatively structured or unstructured.[11] Determining a mayor's task structure requires gauging the city's most pressing problems as to their degree of analyzability, the degree of availability of ready solutions, including appropriate resources to ameliorate these problems, and the degree of consensus among decision-makers and relevant groups about means and preferred outcomes.[12] When tasks are structured, they are analyzable, consensus exists about both means and ends, and solutions and resources are available to accomplish them.

Faced with structured tasks, a mayor can effectively direct his activities toward articulating the latent agreement in the community about the need for solving a widely recognized problem and marshaling the resources necessary to alleviate it. In contrast, unstructured tasks are not readily amenable to analysis, have no obvious solutions, and the community lacks both resources for possible remedies and consensus about preferred means and ends. It is hypothesized that the more structured the tasks in a mayor's task environment, the more favorable the situation for mayoral leadership.

The *position power* of the mayoral role includes the formal and informal political resources a community bestows upon the office of mayor. Formal powers include legal powers, like a four-year term, budget-making authority, an item veto, and the power to appoint department heads without city council approval. Informal powers include the availability of political parties and an ethos that a mayor should initiate innovations. It is hypothesized that the more position power inherent in the mayoral role, the more favorable the situation for mayoral leadership initiatives.

Combining these three situational characteristics produces a continuum that allows communities to be ordered by their degree of favorableness to mayoral leadership. For purposes of this sketch, situations will be divided into only three classes: favorable, mixed, and unfavorable. Favorable situations are hypothesized to be contexts with pluralistic interorganizational relations, structured tasks, and strong mayoral position power. In contrast, unfavorable situations are hypothesized to be contexts with polarized interorganizational relations, unstructured tasks, and weak mayoral position power. In between are mixed situations that are high on one or two dimensions and low on others or fall somewhere between the polls on all three dimensions; for example, pluralistic polities with unstructured tasks and weak mayoral position power.

This ordering of situations is speculative; systematic testing needs to be undertaken to substantiate its validity. Nevertheless, other contingency theories of leadership effectiveness and previous studies of mayoral leadership offer some initial support for this ordering.[13] For example, New Haven in the 1950s provided Mayor Lee a pluralistic polity, a structured task (urban renewal), and strong mayoral position power.[14] Cleveland in the late 1960s, on the other hand, provided Mayor Stokes polarized interorganizational relations, unstructured problems (race relations and poverty), and a relatively weak mayoral office.

Style Factors

The other major subsystem in a leadership system is the individual. The individual interacts with his task environment through a set of behaviors rooted in his *leadership style,* defined by Fiedler as "the underlying need structure of the individual which motivates his behavior in various leadership situations."[15] This definition of leadership style is significant, because "important leadership behaviors of the same individual differ from situation to situation, while the need-structure which motivates these behaviors may be seen as constant."[16] This means that while a leader's behavior may appear flexible, he has a dominant pattern of behavior that he uses most frequently and particularly in situations with great amounts of stress.

Behavioral research has identified a continuum of leadership styles that allows for the location of an individual's dominant pattern of leadership behavior on the continuum and for the prediction of the effectiveness of different leadership styles in different contexts.[17] The leadership style continuum is anchored at opposite polls by instrumental and expressive orientations, i.e., by task and relationship orientations.[18] The instrumental orientation is characterized by emphasis on goal attainment and work facilitation, with little emphasis put on support and interaction facilitation. The expressive style configuration reverses these tendencies, stressing support and interaction facilitation while devoting little attention to goal attainment or work facilitation. Fiedler describes the task-oriented style as "controlling, active, structuring leadership" as opposed to the relationship-oriented style, described as "permissive, passive, and considerate leadership."[19] While these two social action orientations can appear separately or in combination in actual behavior, the dominant style of a leader will tend toward one end or the other of the continuum.

The dichotomization of cognitive orientations into instrumental and expressive types can be extended to encompass a number of other theoretical constructs without doing undue violence to their original intent.[20] For example, in their discussions of purposive strategies for achieving social change through political action, Warren and Hyman distinguish between collaborative and contest strategies,[21] Walton contrasts power and attitude change strategies,[22] and Riker differentiates between minimum and maximum winning coalitional arrangements.[23] By stretching the instrumental and expressive orientations to include these three typologies of sociopolitical action, the social psychological and small-group nature of the original construct is extended to encompass findings from larger political arenas.[24] While a great deal of research needs to be undertaken to establish the validity of lumping these strategic orientations together, the parallels between them are sufficiently compelling to warrant their tentative inclusion in a hypothetical contingency theory of mayoral leadership. Briefly, it is hypothesized that the instrumentally oriented leader will tend to adopt contest, power, and minimum winning coalition strategies in pursuing change, while the expressively oriented leader will tend to adopt collaborative, attitude change, and maximal winning coalition strategies.

Effectiveness

The final index needed for a contingency theory of mayoral leadership is a measure of effectiveness. The measurement of mayoral effectiveness requires a multidimensional index of manipulative capability; the more closely a mayor is able to manipulate his task environment to approximate his preferred state of affairs, the greater his effectiveness. The literature on mayoral leadership reviewed in chapters 2 and 3 suggested that four variables comprise an index of manipulative capability: the extent to which a mayor is able to mobilize, integrate, and centralize resources and decision-making power, and his ability to innovate.[25] Effective leadership is characterized by high scores on these four factors and is most likely produced when an appropriate leadership style is used in a favorable situation.

In figure 8-1 a contingency model of mayoral leadership effectiveness is created by combining the three analytic indexes of styles, situations, and effectiveness. Following Fiedler's research on small work groups, evidence presented in the three case studies in chapters 4, 5, and 6, and impressions gleaned from a variety of empirical and analytic studies of political leadership, the relationship between style, situation, and effective leadership is hypothesized to be curvilinear. In other words, it is hypothesized that in the most favorable and the least favorable leadership situations, an instrumental leadership style will tend to be more effective

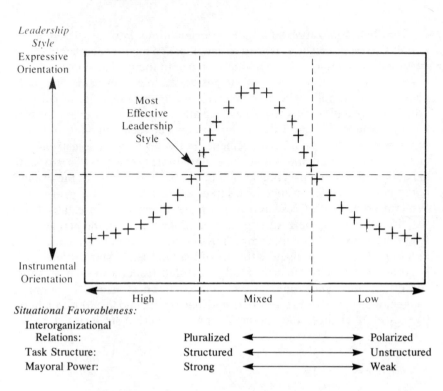

Leadership Style
Expressive Orientation

Most Effective Leadership Style →

Instrumental Orientation

High | Mixed | Low

Situational Favorableness:

Interorganizational Relations:	Pluralized ← →	Polarized
Task Structure:	Structured ← →	Unstructured
Mayoral Power:	Strong ← →	Weak

+ + + + = Trace line of the hypothetical distribution of the means of the most effective leadership style for each point on the continuum of situational favorableness.

Figure 8-1. A Contingency Model of Effective Mayoral Leadership

than an expressive leadership style; but in intermediately favorable (mixed) situations, a leader with an expressive orientation will tend to have a greater manipulative capability than a leader with an instrumental style.

These hypotheses are based on the following line of analysis: In the most favorable leadership situations—where interorganizational relations are pluralized, tasks are structured, and mayoral power is high—a mayor can use his considerable powers to attack acknowledged problems with well-accepted strategies in an environment that is supportive of various forms of bargaining and negotiating. Even when a mayor engages in few expressive activities, there will be enough communitywide agreement on the tasks to be accomplished and on the legitimacy of the mayor to promote solutions that he will have wide support. When the mayor has substantial power and an instrumental orientation, he will be able to mobilize resources easily and apply them to innovative programs. In situations that are highly favorable to leadership initiatives, instrumentally oriented mayors will tend to outperform relationship oriented mayors, because relationships are so favorable to leadership initiatives that expressive behavior will merely reinforce favorable attitudes toward change, be redundant, while instrumental efforts will tend to produce task-related results.

In the least favorable situations—when a community is polarized, tasks are unstructured, and mayoral power is weak—a mayor with an instrumentally oriented leadership style can be a welcome relief from immobilism. Under these conditions, an expressively oriented mayor may spend all his time building a consensus and reacting to conflict rather than manipulating his environment. An instrumentally oriented mayor, on the other hand, will often push ahead toward a goal regardless of the impact of his actions on his popularity. He will do *something* even if he excludes some interests and even if he makes some enemies.

In mixed situations a mayor with an expressive leadership style is likely to be more effective than an instrumentally oriented mayor because the ambiguity of the situation makes effective cooperation problematic, yet enough goodwill and task structure exists to build a moderate degree of consensus. Under these conditions, a mayor who is committed to consensus building can have substantial success, but a mayor who is predominantly instrumentally oriented can exacerbate antagonisms causing distrust, immobilism, and low levels of effectiveness.

A number of corollaries can be generated by refining this sketch of a contingency theory, but rigorous research and in-depth analysis needs to be undertaken to fully exploit its potential ramifications. The intention of this discussion has been to outline the major features of a contingency theory of mayoral effectiveness, not to elaborate on all its dimensions. But irrespective of the tentative nature of this sketch, some pragmatic implications of a contingency theory of mayoral effectiveness can be explicated. Hopefully, the potential contribution of a more detailed contingency theory of mayoral effectiveness will help make contingency modeling an attractive area for more rigorous research in the future.

Implications of a Contingency Theory for Mayoral Practice

A carefully developed and rigorously tested contingency theory of mayoral leadership can affect mayoral practice through: job engineering, mayoral recruitment and selection, and the design of mayoral leadership strategies. Such spillovers of theory into practice help unify administrative theory and practice. The following discussion, while hardly exhaustive, briefly suggests the utility of a contingency theory for administrative practice.

Job Engineering

A major strategy for improving leadership effectiveness is to increase the favorableness of the situation.[26] By changing characteristics of the situation, it is possible to make it more responsive to mayoral leadership initiatives. Altering the structure of urban polities to affect mayoral leadership has been a well-accepted strategy in municipal polities. The history of the municipal reform movement supports this assertion. Issues like metropolitan government, neighborhood control, the city manager movement, and the merit system involved the role of the mayor and his ability to influence community affairs. Through the use of the framework provided by this contingency model of mayoral leadership, we can trace the probable consequences of similar reform proposals and identify possible secondary and unanticipated consequences associated with novel proposals. This is no small advance in efforts to expand our knowledge of urban political dynamics. A few examples of contingency thinking will serve to support this approach.

One currently popular proposal for restructuring interorganizational relations involves neighborhood control of certain urban services. In this case the political situation would be changed from centralized to decentralized decision making within semiautonomous and relatively homogeneous units of government.[27] By decentralizing decision making, the immobilism of the central government caused by polarization can be replaced by the responsiveness of the more local unit to particular neighborhood needs. Under these conditions, a mayor may be able to promote innovations by bargaining separately with local neighborhood councils, because the community as a whole would be changed from an immobilized polity at one decision-making center to a pluralistic polity of homogeneous enclaves with multiple decision making centers.

Another example of structural reform affecting situational favorableness involves the structure of local government tasks. By transferring unstructured problems like poverty and pollution to higher levels of government, a mayor can be left with more structured and solvable local problems, like those that concern physical change and service distribution. To the extent that unstructured problems confront local government with problematic preferences, unclear technologies, and fluid clienteles, mayoral leadership efforts will be exhausted by continuous problems of secondary and unintended consequences.[28] Therefore, restructuring the configuration of local government tasks can simplify and focus a mayor's leadership job.

Increasing mayoral power is another way to improve a situation's favorableness. Jurisdictions seeking more executive leadership might increase the legal powers of the mayoralty. A mayor might be armed with veto powers, the authority to independently appoint department heads, a four-year term, and partisan elections. Strengthening mayoral power through structural reforms has been a well-accepted method of improving mayoral leadership, but even without changes in the task environment of the mayoral job, contingency thinking can still improve mayoral performance by influencing mayoral recruitment and selection.

Mayoral Recruitment and Selection

Many successful and ambitious people mistakenly assume that all situations are equally malleable, and that their leadership style will work equally well in all contexts. The sad experience of formerly successful business executives performing ineffectively in mayoral roles provides valuable lessons on the error of this reasoning.[29] Similarly, frustrated mayors occasionally proclaim their city to be ungovernable.[30] But they are probably overlooking the possibility that their style may be inappropriate for their city and that another person with another leadership style might be able to make the city governable.

The contingency approach may prevent agonizing mismatches of style and circumstances. Prospective mayoral candidates may think twice before seeking office if their personal style is mismatched with a city's situational configuration. Likewise, city councils may choose city managers on the basis of a candidate's style rather than his experience or reputation. In short, a well-developed contingency theory may appreciably improve mayoral recruitment and selection by making the choices of prospective candidates, nominating bodies, endorsement agencies, and selection committees better informed.

Mayoral Leadership Strategies

Even though a leadership style or orientation is assumed to be relatively unchangeable, an individual, over a short run, can consciously control his reponses to more appropriately fit his behavior to a situation. In urban settings, a mayor may be able to mold his interpersonal style to make it more appropriate to the demands of his situation. This control of interpersonal style is usually fragile and temporary, and may disintegrate under stress or in crisis circumstances.[31] Nevertheless, it may be effective over an extended period of time. The contingency approach may be useful to a mayor with the ability to control his style, because it can provide cues for choosing appropriate behavioral strategies. But in spite of the possibilities for "conscious control," leadership orientations that are skewed strongly toward one pole of the style continuum will be difficult to modify, making "best fit" strategic behavior difficult and often obviously inauthentic.[32]

These implications of a contingency theory for mayoral practice provide justification for continued development of a management science of mayoral leadership. However, before any further progress can be made, some changes must take place in our process of conducting research on mayoral leadership. First, the contingency approach requires a comparative methodology and the abandonment of the case method that has dominated research on mayoral behavior. Second, social scientists must give more attention to forming research hypotheses that have possible implications for mayoral practice, rather than for the sole purpose of sharpening techniques or building theoretical constructs. Finally, students of mayoral leadership must find vehicles to communicate their findings to mayors, prospective mayors, and the general public. This means social scientists will have to write with less methodological elegance and will have to venture from the university to communicate their findings to wider audiences. These changes will not be easy for most political scientists, but should they produce pragmatic knowledge, they will find receptive audiences.

Racial Conflict and the American Mayor: Directions for Future Research

Because racial conflict produces extraordinary problems for mayors, and mayors are called upon to grapple with the most nagging of our urban problems, scholars interested in strengthening local efforts to solve urban problems might profitably focus future research on strategies for making situations more favorable to mayoral leadership initiatives. For example, if interorganizational relations need to be made less polarized and more pluralistic, how does one design a strategy for accomplishing such a task? Are metropolitanization or disannexation feasible solutions to immobilism? What do we know about the conditions and strategies that have produced these structural realignments in American cities? If task structures need to be less ambiguous, and either a devolvement or consolidation of service areas appears to be an appropriate structural reform, how does one move problems up and down or out of the local government's jurisdiction? Finally, if mayoral power needs to be enhanced, what additional power does a mayor need? How does a city go about reforming its government to give its mayor more power? What strategies are likely to work best? Which are likely to fail?

These are just a few of the questions that might be addressed by students interested in strengthening the American mayoralty. They are important issues for action research and can only be intelligently addressed and linked to mayoral performance if an integrated framework is kept in mind. Such a framework desperately needs to be developed, and contingency modeling provides an appropriate and valuable orientation. But a unified research effort can only be attained through agreement among a wide range of students interested in the mayoralty on the goals for research and the central issues, concepts, and approaches to be utilized. So far, no such agreement seems to have emerged.

It is hoped that the suggestions offered here for further research will allow political scientists interested in urban leadership to better serve political leaders, their natural constituency, rather than use political leaders mainly as research subjects. Should such a design trend become popular, political scientists might be able to reenter the world of affairs with something unique to offer rather than function merely as informed citizens. The choice depends, of course, on the inclinations of the individual researcher, but the opportunity for choice depends on the direction of learning. Hopefully, our research direction in this decade will provide us with the opportunity to choose.

Notes

1. An excellent recent review of leadership research is Edwin P. Hollander and James W. Julian, "Contemporary Trends in the Analysis of Leadership Process," *Psychological Bulletin* 71, (1969), pp. 387-97; see also, Ralph M. Stogdill, *Handbook of Leadership: A Survey of Theory and Research* (New York: The Free Press, 1974).

2. The contingency approach used in this chapter is consistent with the spirit of Joan Woodward's *Industrial Organization: Theory and Practice* (London: Oxford University Press, 1965) and Paul R. Lawrence and Jay W. Lorsch's *Organization and Environment: Managing Differentiation and Integration* (Homewood, Ill.: Richard D. Irwin, Inc., 1969), but it is much closer to the work of Fred E. Fiedler and his associates. Fiedler has written extensively on his contingency theory of leadership over the past twenty years, but perhaps the clearest over-all statements of his position and research can be found in: Fred E. Fiedler, *A Theory of Leadership Effectiveness* (New York: McGraw-Hill Book Co., 1967); "Engineer the Job to Fit the Manager," *Harvard Business Review* 43 (1965), pp. 115-22; "Validation and Extension of the Contingency Model of Leadership Effectiveness: A Review of Empirical Findings," *Psychological Bulletin* 76 (1971), pp. 128-48; J. G. Hunt, "Organizational Leadership: Some Theoretical and Empirical Considerations," *Business Perspectives,* (Summer 1968), pp. 16-24; and Martin N. Chemers and Robert W. Rice, "A Theoretical and Empirical Examination of Fiedler's Contingency Model of Leadership Effectiveness," in J.G. Hunt and L.L. Larson (eds.), *Contingency Approaches to Leadership* (Carbondale, Ill.: Southern Illinois University Press, 1974).

3.   See, for example, G. Graen, D. Alvares, J.B. Orris, and J.A. Martella, "The Contingency Model of Leadership Effectiveness: Antecedent and Evidential Results," *Psychological Bulletin* 74 (1970), pp. 285-95; and S. Kerr and A. Harlan, "Predicting the Effects of Leadership Training and Experience from the Contingency Model: Some Remaining Problems," *Journal of Applied Psychology* 57 (1973), pp. 114-17.

4.   Chemers and Rice, "A Theoretical and Empirical Examination of Fiedler's Contingency Model of Leadership Effectiveness," p. 15.

5.   I wish to thank Michael White of Syracuse University for pointing out this distinction. Perhaps the best method for grasping the differences between the study of administration and administrative science is to scan recent issues of the *Administrative Science Quarterly* for examples of the former orientation, and *Management Science* for examples of the latter approach.

6.   The fragmentation of political leadership research into various subspecialties has been examined by Glenn D. Paige in the "Over-view" chapter of his edited volume *Political Leadership* (New York: The Free Press, 1972), especially pp. 8-9.

7.   The effectiveness of the anthropological approach for specifying actual managerial behavior has been recently demonstrated by Henry Mintzberg *The Nature of Managerial Work* (New York: Harper & Row, Publishers, 1973); and "Managerial Work: Analysis from Observation," *Management Science* 18 (October 1971), pp. 97-110. At present, no comparable study of mayoral behavior exists.

8.   See F.M. Fisher and A. Ando, "Two Theorems on *Ceteris Paribus* in the Analysis of Dynamic Systems," *American Political Science Review* 56 (March 1962), pp. 103-13, for an application of the concept of near decomposability to political analysis.

9.   Herbert A. Simon, *The Sciences of the Artificial* (Cambridge, Mass.: M.I.T. Press, 1969), p. 100.

10.   For fuller discussions of the importance of the configuration of the interorganizational relations to mayoral leadership, see Wen H. Kuo, "Mayoral Influence in Urban Policy Making," *American Journal of Sociology* 79 (1973), pp. 620-38.

11.   The idea of structure is taken from Fiedler; see *A Theory of Leadership Effectiveness,* pp. 25-28.

12.   This approach to specifying the properties of "task structures" is more political than Fiedler's and is largely drawn from James D. Thompson's *Organizations in Action* (New York: McGraw-Hill Book Co., 1967), pp. 134-35.

13. See Charles H. Levine and Clifford Kaufman, "Urban Conflict as a Constraint on Mayoral Leadership: Lessons from Gary and Cleveland," *American Politics Quarterly* 2 (January 1974), pp. 78-106.

14. See Robert A. Dahl, *Who Governs?* (New Haven: Yale University Press, 1961).

15. Fiedler, *A Theory of Leadership Effectiveness,* p. 36.

16. Ibid.

17. See Stogdill, *Handbook of Leadership,* pp. 128-42 for a discussion of this research.

18. See David G. Bowers and Stanley E. Seashore, "Predicting Organizational Effectiveness with a Four-Factor Theory of Leadership," *Administrative Science Quarterly,* (1966), pp. 238-63; for a more sociological discussion of these orientations, see Amitai Etzioni, "Dual Leadership in Complex Organizations," *American Sociological Review* 30 (1965), pp. 688-98.

19. See Fiedler, "Engineering the Job to Fit the Manager."

20. The works cited here by Warren and Hyman, Walton, and Riker share a common concern with purposive social change under conditions of communal conflict.

21. Roland L. Warren and Herbert H. Hyman, "Purposive Community Change in Consensus and Dissensus Situations." in Terry N. Clark (ed.) *Community Structure and Decision Making: Comparative Analyses* (San Francisco: Chandler Publishing Company, 1968), pp. 407-24.

22. Richard E. Walton, "Two Strategies of Social Change and their Dilemmas," *Journal of Applied Behavioral Science* 7 (1965), pp. 167-79.

23. William H. Riker, *The Theory of Political Coalitions* (New Haven: Yale University Press, 1962).

24. While most usages of the instrumental-expressive dichotomy have tended to focus on leadership in small groups and have stressed cognitive styles rather than strategic behavior, it is not unreasonable to extend the typology to encompass leadership behavior in large-scale systems. One recent example of typological analysis of political leaders that bears some relationship to the analysis used here is James D. Barber, *The Presidential Character* (Englewood Cliffs, N.J.: Prentice-Hall, Inc., 1972).

25. See chapter Two, notes 26 through 34.

26. See Fiedler, "Engineer the Job to Fit the Manager."

27. See Milton Kotler, *Neighborhood Government* (Indianapolis: Bobbs-Merrill Co., 1969); and, Joseph F. Zimmerman, *The Federated City* (New York: St. Martins Press, 1972).

28. See Michael D. Cohen, James G. March, and Johan P. Olsen, ''A Garbage Can Model of Organizational Choice,'' *Administrative Science Quarterly* 17 (March 1972), pp. 1-25.

29. For a discussion of this phenomena, see Jeffrey L. Pressman, ''Preconditions of Mayoral Leadership,'' *American Political Science Review* 66 (June 1972), pp. 511-24.

30. See ''The Mayor of Los Angeles Cross Examined,'' in Leonard I. Ruchelman, (ed.) *Big City Mayors* (Bloomington, Ind.: Indiana University Press, 1969), pp. 296-320.

31. See Robert L. Kahn, Donald M. Wolfe, Robert P. Quinn, J. Diedrick Snock, and Robert A. Rosenthal, *Organizational Stress: Studies in Role Conflict and Ambiguity* (New York: John Wiley & Sons, 1964); and Russell L. Ackoff and Fred E. Emery, *On Purposeful Systems* (Chicago: Aldine-Atherton, Inc., 1972).

32. For a review of ''authenticity'' in organizational settings, see Robert T. Golembiewski, *Renewing Organizations* (Itasca, Ill.: F.E. Peacock Publishers, 1972), pp. 222-24.

Index

Index

Addonisio, Hugh, 119
Administrative science, 129-131
Arrington, Richard, Jr., 97

Backoff, Robert, xii
Banfield, Edward C., 11
Barber, James, 18
Barr, Joseph, 18
Bauer, Cecil, 95
Behavior: administrative, 129; mayoral, 6-7, 139-140
Bennis, Warren, 12
Birmingham, Alabama, xi, xii, 6, 85-103, 109-113, 123; 1967 mayoral election, 85, 91-92; reform movement in, 86-87; government of, 87-88; electoral politics of, 89-94; 1971 mayoral election, 92; development of a progressive bloc in, 93; Birmingham Action Group (BAG), 93; Operation New Birmingham (ONB), 93-98, 101; Community Affairs Committee (CAC), 94-98, 101; leadership structure in, 94-98; effects of Seibels's administration, 98-103; power structure in, 113-114; mayoral effectiveness in, 114-115
Birmingham Action Group (BAG), 93
Boone, Charles, 80
Boutwell, Albert, 89, 92, 94, 98; 1963 mayoral race, 90-91; 1967 mayoral race, 91

Carroll, James, xii
Carney, James, 59-60

Cleveland, Ohio, xi, xii, 109-112, 123; politics in, 6; government of, 53; Democratic Party of, 53; power structure of, 54; and Mayor Locher, 54-55; election of Frank Lausche, 55; growth of black population in, 56; 1965 mayoral election, 56-57; 1967 mayoral election, 57-58; 1969 mayoral election, 58-59; 1971 mayoral election, 59-60; "Cleveland: NOW!", 60-61, 110; and Carl Stokes's administration, 60-65; power structure of, 113-114; mayoral effectiveness in, 114-115
Community Affairs Committee (CAC), 94-98, 101
Conner, Theophilus Eugene "Bull", 86, 89, 97; 1963 mayoral race, 90-91

Consociation, 43-46; democracy, 44
Cunningham, James V., 11, 18

Dahl, Robert A., 11, 16
Daley, Richard, 18, 119
Davis, Benjamin O., 63
Democracy, 44
Diamant, Alfred, xii
Dill, Richard, 91

Edinger, Lewis, 12-13
Effectiveness, mayoral, 6-7, 35, 135-137; dominant model of, 14-21; goals and, 19-20; in Birmingham, Cleveland, and Gary, 114-115; strategy for improving, 137-140
Entrepreneur, civic, 16-18

Farmer, Richard, xii
Fiedler, Fred E., 128, 134

Garofoli, Anthony, 59, 61, 62
Gary, Indiana, xi, xii, 109-112, 123; politics in, 6; government of, 69-70; electoral politics of, 70-73; 1967 mayoral race, 71-72; 1971 mayoral race, 73; Hatcher administration in, 73-81; power structure in, 113-114; mayoral effectiveness in, 114-115
Gaston, A.G., 94, 97
George, Alexander, 11
Goals: and mayoral effectiveness, 19-20
Greenstone, J. David, 11
Gruenberg, Barry, 119

Hahn, Harlan, xii
Haines, Arthur J., 90, 92
Hatcher, Richard, xi, 69, 109, 113-114, 116, 119, 123, 130; his election to Gary City Council, 71; 1967 mayoral race, 71-72; 1971 mayoral race, 73; administration of, 73-81; programs of, 78-79; and police department changes, 80; and education, 80-81
Hilton, James, 80
Hodges, Judson, 102
Holland, R. William, xii
Holloway, Harry, 89
Hyman, Herbert H., 135
Hyneman, Charles, xii

Iverson, Robert, xii

147

Johnson, Lyndon B., 62, 77, 122

Katz, A. Martin, 70-71, 77; and 1967 mayoral
    race, 71-72
Kaufman, Clifford, xii, 1
Kelly, Robert J., 58-59
King, Martin Luther, 60, 80, 89; his
    description of Birmingham, 85
King, Tom, 90
Klementowicz, Bronis, 55
Konrady, Bernard, 72
Kotter, John P., 11
Krupa, John G., 72

Langer, Earl, 91
Lausche, Frank, 55
Lawrence, Paul R., 11
Leadership: concept of, 12-14; as an
    entrepreneurial task, 15; success, 16;
    structures, 20-21; models, 35-36,
    41-43; executive, 45; research,
    127-129
Leadership, mayoral, 3-5, 11; and racial
    conflict, 3-7; study of, 5-6;
    methodology and, 6-7, 12-14;
    dominant model of, 11-12; as a
    structure of influence, 14-15; as
    entrepreneurship, 16-18; limits of,
    21-25; and racial polarization, 22-25;
    contingency theory of, 131-137
Leadership models, 35-36, 41-43
Leadership styles, 12, 18-19, 22, 134-135
Lee, Richard, 16, 18, 22, 134
Levine, E. Lester, xii
Levine, Elaine, xii
Lipjhart, Arend, 7, 43, 44
Locher, Ralph, 18, 54-55; and 1965 mayoral
    election, 56-67; and 1967 mayoral
    election, 57-58
Lowi, Theodore, 11

Maier, Henry, 119
Mayoral behavior, See Behavior
Mayoral effectiveness, See Effectiveness,
    mayoral
Mayoral leadership, See Leadership,
    mayoral
Mayoral performance, See Performance,
    mayoral
Mayoral recruitment, See Recruitment,
    mayoral
Mayoral selection, See Selection, mayoral
Mayoral succession, See Succession,
    mayoral
Mayors, 13; leadership ability of, 13-14;
    effectiveness of, 6-7, 14-21; goals of,
    19-20; entrepreneurial skills of, 20;

and leadership structures, 20-21;
    limits of leadership of, 21-25; black,
    116-117; task structures of, 133; and
    racial conflict, 141-142
McAllister, Ralph, 56-57
McFarland, Andrew S., 22
McNair, Chris, 97
Moore, Jamie, 97, 99
Murphy, Thomas, xii

Nigro, Lloyd, xii
Nixon, Richard M., 77, 122

Operation New Birmingham (ONB), 93-98,
    101
Opportunity Structures, 39-41

Parsons, Thomas, 99
Pavlock, René, xii
Performance, mayoral, 22; assessment of, 16
Perk, Ralph, 56-57, 65; and 1969 mayoral
    race, 58-59; and 1971 mayoral race,
    59-60
Perry, James, xii
Peterson, Paul E., 11
Pinckney, Arnold R., 59-60, 65
Pitts, Lucius, 95
Polarization, community, 43
Polarization, racial, 35-37, 81, 111; and
    mayoral leadership, 22-25
Politics, city, 11
Power structures, 6; in Birmingham,
    Cleveland, and Gary, 113-114
Pressman, Jeffrey, xii, 19, 35
Psychology, social, 12

Radigan, Joseph B., 72
Recruitment, mayoral, 6, 139; patterns of,
    39-40
Regimes, consociational, 43-46
Rhodes, Jim, 57
Rogers, David, 11
Role conflict, 22
Rossi, Peter, xi

Salisbury, Robert H., 11, 17
Sayre, Wallace S., 11
Schuman, Howard, 119
Seibels, George, Jr., 90, 109, 113-114; his
    1967 election, 85, 91-92; his 1971
    election, 92; criticisms of, 96-97;
    achievements and failures of, 98-103
Selection, mayoral, 139
Shores, Arthur, 93, 94, 97
Siffen, William, xii
Stability, political, 3
Stanton, James, 59, 61, 62

Stinchcombe, Arthur, 15
Stokes, Carl, xi, 53, 55, 109, 111, 113-114, 116, 119, 123, 134; 1965 campaign strategy of, 56-57; 1967 campaign of, 57-58; 1969 campaign of, 58-59; and 1971 mayoral race, 59-60; administration of, 61-65
Stone, Clarence, xii
Succession, mayoral, 39-40
Systems, political: pluralized, 37-39, 41-43; polarized, 37-39

Taft, Seth, 57-59
Thayer, Frederick, xii

Townsend, S. Vincent, 90, 95

Van den Berghe, Pierre L., 36

Waggoner, J.D., 90
Waldo, Dwight, xii
Wallace, George, 88
Warren, Roland L., 135
Washington, Walter, 119
Whelan, Robert, xii
White, Michael, xii
Wilbern, York, xii
Williams, Dr. Alexander, 73

Young, George, 91, 92

About the Author

Charles H. Levine is Assistant Professor of Public Administration at the Maxwell School of Citizenship and Public Affairs, Syracuse University. A graduate of the University of Connecticut, Mr. Levine received M.B.A., M.P.A., and Ph.D. degrees from Indiana University. He previously taught at Indiana, Michigan State University, and the University of Maryland before joining the Syracuse faculty as Assistant Director of the Maxwell Midcareer Program. Mr. Levine has been a Ford Foundation Faculty Fellow at the Federal Executive Institute and a Research Associate of the National Academy of Public Administration and is currently an associate of the Indiana University International Development Research Center. He is presently serving as coeditor of *Administration and Society* and is engaged in research on administrative behavior and organizational design.